A Matter of Honour

A Matter of Honour

Experiences of Turkish Women Immigrants

Tahire Kocturk

Zed Books Ltd
London and New Jersey

A Matter of Honour: Experiences of Turkish Women Immigrants was first published by
Zed Books Ltd, 57 Caledonian Road, London N1 9BU, United Kingdom and
165 First Avenue, Atlantic Highlands, New Jersey 07716, United States of America,
in 1992

Copyright © Tahire Kocturk, 1992

Cover designed by Sophie Buchet
Typeset by EMS Photosetters, Thorpe Bay, Essex
Printed and bound in the United Kingdom
by WBC Ltd., Bridgend, Mid Glamorgan

ISBN 1 85649 075 0 Hb
1 85649 076 9 Pb

UK CIP is available from British Library
US CIP is available from the Library of Congress

Contents

Acknowledgements

The study, 'Family and Gender Relations among Muslim Immigrants in Sweden', was carried out between June 1986 and October 1989. The project received financial support from the Delegation for Social Research (DSF) of the Swedish Social Department (Socialdepartementet). It was carried out through the Sociological Institute of Göteborgs University. Rita Liljeström was the project leader.

Many people assisted me during the different phases of the study. A sociologist, Yasemin Basgul, and a lawyer, Ihsan Dogan, gave valuable assistance collecting material, through interviewing some of the subjects and transcribing the recorded material. Fifty-nine Turkish immigrants generously offered to share their experiences and opinions, which were of vital importance to the project. Birgit Jörn provided assistance translating some of the material into Swedish, as well as in the administration of the project. Lena Strömqvist from the DSF and Birgitta Ornbrant from the Delegation for Immigrant Research (DEIFO) gave me moral support. A long-standing personal friend, John E. Stark, aided me greatly in my effort to express myself correctly and intelligibly in a foreign language. John E. Stark, Björn Ericsson, Ann-Madlen Gelotte and Rita Liljeström contributed valuable comments about the presentation, which greatly facilitated the editorial work. My husband, Karl, and my children, Bugra and Deniz, gave me their cheerful and patient support during the many hours I spent sitting in front of a keyboard.

I am grateful for all the support I have received which has made this book possible.

Introduction

Strange things happen when one becomes an 'immigrant'. Living and working in a foreign country was not a new experience for me; I had visited other countries before and returned home with pleasant impressions. Once I decided to settle down in Sweden ten years ago, however, I noticed that I suddenly began 'watching' myself in a way I had never done before. I wanted to understand and explain every move I made, every thought that crossed my mind. I also expected explanations from others. I frequently asked seemingly silly questions. Differences in coffee drinking, for instance, could be an issue for me ('why do Swedes drink such strong coffee so often, and why do we boil ours while they filter theirs?'). I wondered why being a tourist was a pleasant experience while emigration, which theoretically should be even more exciting, produced doubts and fears. Did it have something to do with a time factor? Did it have anything to do with the fact that a tourist knows he or she will return to familiar places in the future, while an immigrant takes the risk of never returning? But a future risk should not produce such great anxiety, I thought, because after all, life involves taking risks.

I began thinking that the past dimension of time is probably more important. The difference between a tourist and an immigrant may be that the tourist does not have to worry about losing his or her history, while an immigrant feels that the past will perhaps be sacrificed. On the one hand, there is the magic formula: 'The sooner I forget the old, the quicker I learn the new, the better I adapt.' But the prospect of suppressing history is extremely anxiety producing – almost like treason. I think it is this fear of the impossible task of losing contact with one's past that lies at the root of an immigrant's need to explain: in order to adapt to the new, one must carefully define the old. Things must first be placed in the past so they can be projected into the future, so that they make sense. Things can be explained and understood once they are placed into a context. The context of cultural phenomena is history.

I went around for a long time feeling the need to say, 'but Turks do have a history, you know; Turks do have a personality – it can be explained. We were not just planted here.' I talked in this vein with a lot of people, both Europeans and Turks. I wanted to know how other Turks felt. Women's perspectives were particularly interesting to me. In time, I began feeling a great need to tell the story of Turkish women, so that this story could also be placed somewhere in the context of women's experiences in Europe. I am not, of course, the first to write about Turkish women or about the Turkish immigrant experience. There was a need to collect the various studies and observations that give clues in a volume which could tell the story to Europeans. My need to tell about ourselves grew each time I faced well-meaning generalizations or had to stand up against less friendly prejudices. A particularly upsetting incident experienced by a woman I met – which I mention in the last section of this book – convinced me that this story must be compiled soon. I felt it was so urgent that I temporarily interrupted a career in the natural sciences in order to summarize some of the main points of our cultural baggage, to compile the works of others, to hear people tell me about their life in a European country, and write about it, in an attempt to make the voices of Turkish women heard. This book is the result of that attempt.

Telling a history is complicated for women, because history generally tells the story of men. Accounts about women are few, if not impossible to find. In the case of Turkey it is very difficult to find anything directly said or done by ordinary women. But I do not consider this a great hindrance as women can learn much about themselves by first studying their men. The seemingly very striking differences between Turkish/'Muslim' and Western/'Christian' women is a popular subject for comparison. I often think that many insights into the human condition can be gained by comparing the men these societies have produced. Differences in the appearance of women in Muslim and Western societies, I believe, reflect to a greater extent the different ideals of the men than the intrinsic dissimilarity in the constitution of the women.

An amusing exercise can be to compare the male heroes popularly described in the literature and films of the respective societies. The traditional Western European male hero is a Casanova type, who later evolves into a lonely cowboy, or a daring super-spy. These are unattached men who, as they go through life, meet and seduce women along the way as if engaging in a favourite hobby. After passionate encounters in these films, the Western hero is often depicted disappearing on his horse or in an airplane towards new horizons, to pursue new adventures. These men always leave behind an assortment of women grateful for ever having been loved by them. Most of us remember the philosophy about women articulated in the John Wayne films of the 1960s to 'love 'em and leave 'em'. The male heroes in the European/'Christian' culture treat women as free people, basically capable of taking care of themselves, with sporadic manifestations of sexual affection from men.

Compared to the lonely cowboy, the popular Middle Eastern hero is either a rich and handsome prince or a revolutionary. Instead of being a lonely drifter, the 'Muslim' always has a family, headed by a powerful mother, behind him. Once he loves a woman, he never disappears from her life. The Middle Eastern hero instead captures her, takes her with him to his home and deposits her in some type of a harem, or under the care of his family. He never lets his woman go: he is supposed to sustain a formidable possessiveness and to demand her absolute attachment, forever. If Western/'Christian' male heroes treat women as free sexual playthings, for the Middle Eastern/'Muslim' hero women are sexual captives. Neither of these images are complimentary to women. But where do these images originate from? The origins may be found in the traditions and ideologies that have played a role in the formation of gender roles within the primary organization where these take shape, the family.

The family structure west of a line drawn between St Petersburg and Trieste has been different from the Eastern family (Utrio, 1987). The Western family has historically been a 'nuclear' family, where couples got married at a relatively late stage in their lives and had fewer children. Even though society was strongly patriarchal and exerted pressure on women to limit reproduction through their biological fate, the requirement for high fertility was not strong. Christian ideology does not consider celibacy a sin. Significant numbers of people did not marry in some European societies. Liljeström (1982) points out that as much as 37–40% of upper class women in the mid-1800s in Sweden were never married. Premarital relations were frowned upon, but to be a virgin at marriage was not an absolute requirement. In her study of gender relations in Sweden, Liljeström (1982) notes that as many as a third of rural girls were pregnant at marriage. Women who had acquired sexual experience were not as strongly stigmatized as in 'Muslim' societies.

Strict segregation of genders was not practised within the European family or society. Women mingled in public areas much more freely and many could enter professions. According to Utrio (1987), women in European societies were represented in the guilds by the 1300s. It was relatively common for some women to perform work outside their own homes until they got married in their late twenties; rural girls between the ages of 15 and 17 were sent out to work as maids on farms. With industrialization, some young girls left home for the factories or the cities. Upper class girls sometimes worked as teachers, nurses, governesses or clerks. Other bourgeois women sometimes got parental permission to travel and engage in intellectual endeavours before getting married (Liljeström, 1982). Simply having come into contact with life outside the confines of their homes was not as great a 'shame' for Western women as it has been for Middle Eastern women. As European women were free to go out in public, some gained sexual experience which, if manipulated correctly, did not necessarily lead to their becoming social outcasts. Women who had children outside marriage could, for instance, leave them at orphanages or in the care of others, and still get married later on. Such routes have, until recently, been closed to Muslim women. In the Western family, there was also greater tolerance of women working after marriage. A working woman's husband was considered a financial failure, but an inability to provide enough to keep his wife and children in absolute confinement did not necessarily cast a shadow on the man's moral integrity. When it became necessary, with industrialization, for large numbers of women to combine their home-based activities with outside work, women faced great practical difficulties, but this was not considered to be an infringement of social mores as would have been the case in Muslim cultures. The mechanisms of the suppression of women in Western societies have been very different to those in Eastern/'Muslim' societies.

The Middle Eastern/'Muslim' family has traditionally been a large unit encompassing several generations, where relations between family members consisted of well-defined rights and responsibilities. Sexual behaviour has been considered a social responsibility rather than a matter of romantic personal choice. Sexuality was strictly regulated by the family. Couples were married at the time of puberty: celibacy and non-marital relations were condemned. Gender roles were segregated into the private and public spheres of life. All women's activities were strictly confined to the private sphere – to the home and family. In principle women were not supposed to leave their homes for any purpose. A working woman endangered the moral reputation of her husband and brothers. Gender segregation was sanctioned by the traditions of Islam, which further structured it into law, totally prohibiting each gender from sharing the sphere assigned to the other. It has been more difficult for people from this background to adjust to the industrial labour market. Industry needs individuals with a high degree of physical and psychological mobility: men and women who can leave their own spheres of influence in order to concentrate on the tasks at hand, mixing freely in the sphere traditionally allocated to the opposite sex without worrying about what happens to their gender-specific morality.

Despite the traditional restrictions on women appearing in public, an ever-increasing number of Middle Eastern/'Muslim' women have, since the 1930s, been escaping the confinement of their homes, often working side by side with men, sometimes attaining important public positions. Since the 1960s, significant numbers of Middle Eastern women have also been working in foreign countries.

Turks are a people from a Middle Eastern, semi-agrarian, Muslim society who have had to adjust to an industrialized world, while protecting some of the values they consider to be important. In the following pages the options for change within given traditional and cultural limits are described. Particular emphasis is given to the position of women within the family. The first three chapters offer general background information, necessary for a better understanding of the disparate heritage in the Turkish cultural baggage.

One of the shortcomings of studies on immigrants is that many researchers do not have immigrant backgrounds, do not have the knowledge, do not feel the need or cannot find the time to study extensively the historical processes that lead to certain cultural practices. Much immigrant research relies on observations of the situation of immigrants and how their cultural norms differ from those of the host country. Descriptions which lack a historical perspective can make the behaviour of immigrants seem exotic and incomprehensible. It is only with historical perspective that cultural differences can be satisfactorily explained and the immigrant can be seen, not as a person with bizarre behaviour patterns, but as a human being. An understanding of the status of women through different periods of Turkish history is necessary information, on which this book is built. It is summarily presented in the first chapter.

The mechanisms to suppress women are inextricably bound up with the ideologies which determine sexual conduct in a society. The second chapter presents some of the basics of Islamic teaching on women and the honour ethic – two concepts that overlap – with their effects on the formation of gender roles. Islamic teaching not only defines the ideology surrounding Turkish women, but also that of other Muslim immigrants in Europe, such as Iranian, Arab and Pakistani women. The honour ethic, which is also explained in the second chapter, is a transcultural moral concept which has now become obsolete in many Western European societies but which still has a profound influence on the behaviour of some Mediterranean peoples, regardless of religious background. The lives of Yugoslavian, Greek, Assyrian and Armenian women are just as much influenced by the honour ethic as are their Muslim sisters.

The third chapter is an overview of the status of women in different socio-economic groups in contemporary Turkey. This chapter explains the side-by-side existence and behaviour of modern and traditional women in Turkish society. It is hoped that these first three chapters will facilitate reading the fourth and fifth chapters which, respectively, describe the immigration experience and the Turkish immigrant family in Europe. The fourth chapter is a compilation of studies concerning a new epoch in Turkish history that began in the 1960s: the massive emigration of Turks into Europe as cheap labour. This chapter gives more space to studies of Turkish men. Studies of Turkish immigrant women are rare, due partly to the fact that it is extremely difficult for male researchers to approach Turkish women. Only woman researchers with an appreciable understanding of the history and culture can work with Turkish women. The few studies involving women in Europe are mentioned and a general overview of the immigrant situation is given. The fifth chapter is a presentation of the results of an explorative study which I carried out among Turkish immigrants living in Sweden. In this chapter, based on case studies, Turks reflect on changes which have occurred in their lives as a result of living in a foreign country.

1. Turks

Turkey is a country at the crossroads between Asia and Europe. It consists of 779,452 square kilometres of land, most of which is situated in Asia Minor, or the Anatolian peninsula, and a smaller part in Thrace, which lies in Europe. Central Anatolia consists of a relatively high plateau (varying in height between 800 and 2000 m) enclosed by a ring of mountains. In the east, the mountain ranges meet at the country's highest peak, the Agri Dagi (Mount Ararat, 5165 m).

Because of its elevated and mountainous topography, there are great climatic variations between the different regions. In the inner regions, the mountainous areas and the northeast, winters are severe, with heavy snowfall and temperatures that, in the east, can fall to –40 degrees centigrade. On the coastline, the climate is milder, with rainy winters and dry, warm summers in the west and south. The Black Sea coastal area is somewhat cooler, with more rainfall throughout the year, which contributes to the growth of beautiful forest lands. In the summer, daytime temperatures are generally high, around 30 degrees during July and August. Temperatures as high as 43 degrees are not uncommon in eastern Turkey.

Economically, Turkey is a developing country with a GNP per capita of $1080 in 1985 (Table 1.1). Economic growth is unevenly distributed among the regions. The Aegean and Thracian regions are the most densely populated and highly developed areas of the country, where industry, commerce and agriculture are most intensive. As one moves eastward, development is less conspicuous. Eastern Anatolia is the poorest region of Turkey (Fisher, 1983).

Personal income in the different regions is also uneven. Rural areas, where 54% of the population live, are clearly disadvantaged compared to highly urbanized areas. Income distribution between social classes is also unequal, with the richest 20% controlling 57% of total GNP, while the poorest 40% controls 12% (Table 1.1). Such factors contribute to the widespread poverty in Turkey, especially in rural areas and in the slums of big cities.

Those who have given their ethnic name to the country, the Turks, are an Asian people originating in southwest Mongolia. Turks began migrating as tribes into Anatolia as well as other parts of the world beginning in the tenth century. The tribes that originally settled in Anatolia constituted a minority in relation to the rest of the population. Through the building of two prominent

Table 1.1. Social statistics, Turkey and Sweden

	Turkey	Sweden
Population, 1986 (millions)	50.3	8.3
Population under 16 (millions), 1986	19.2	1.6
% population urbanized, 1985	46	84
Life expectancy at birth (years), 1985	64	77
GNP per capita (US$), 1985	1080	11890
% share of household income, 1975–85		
Lowest 40%	12	21
Highest 20%	57	42
No. of radio/television receivers per 1000 population, 1985	130/148	868/390
% Adults literate, 1985		
Males	86	
Females	62	

Source: State of the World's Children, UNICEF

states, by the Seljuks and Ottomans, the country gradually became Islamic and Turkish. The majority of the people in modern Turkey would identify themselves as being of Turkish ethnicity. There are other minority groups, the largest of which are the Kurds, Assyrians and Armenians.*

The history of Turkish women has been influenced by a curious legacy of many cultural factors which include the central Asian shaman tradition, the Arab Islamic tradition, and the influences of the Anatolian civilizations. The latter include the Hittite, Hellenist, Roman and the Christian–Byzantine eras. To these may be added the influences of the Balkan region and Europe, which have continued from the Middle Ages (the period of Ottoman expansion) up to the recent labour migration which has resulted in an estimated 2.5 million Turks settling in Europe.

Turks

Turks lived as nomadic tribes in central Asia, in the area south and west of the Altai mountains to the Aral sea, bordering Mongolia and China in the east. Turkish ethnicity is recognized by the use of several dialects of a common Turkish language. It includes the Uzbeks, Kazaks, Turkomen, Tartars, Kirghiz, Ugrians and Azeris presently living in the Soviet republics; the Anatolian Turks; the Turkish-speaking Islamic minorities in the Balkans and Macedonia, as well as non-Islamic groups such as the Gagauz of Hungary (Christian) and the Kazars (Jewish) of Eastern Europe (Pavic, 1988; Akiner, 1986; Bowles, 1977; Menges, 1968).

As is the case with most nomadic peoples, the ancient history of the Turks is obscure. It is presumed that the first Hun Empire (220 BC–AD 216) was established by a Turkish dynasty. Written evidence of Turkish existence occurs first in Chinese documents from the sixth century, where they were referred to as *T'chueh*, and are described as a combative, nomadic people who had established several kingdoms to the west of China. In Mongolian texts, Turks are mentioned as *Turuk*; in Latin and Greek as *Turcae*. The name Turk as such is noted in the *Orkhon* inscriptions discovered by the Orkhon River in Mongolia. These texts, the earliest yet discovered, are written in a Turkish-Oghuz dialect dating to the time of the Gökturk Empire (AD 552–745), which was one of the first sedentary kingdoms established by the Turks. The Orkhon writings describe the re-establishment of the Gökturk state after a defeat of one of its kings. Mention is also made of the Turkish people as nomadic cattle grazers and horseback warriors, which matches the accounts given about them in other Chinese and Mongolian documents (Akiner, 1986; Bowles, 1977; Menges, 1968).

The early Turks were shamanists. Shamanism is a naturalistic religion first noted among the Ural–Altaic peoples from the Bering Strait to the north of Scandinavia, and the native peoples of America and Malaysia. Although shamanistic beliefs have been diluted by the encroachment of the axial religions (Christianity, Buddhism and Islam), some still exist among peoples who have adapted to the later religions. Shamanists believe that certain people with supernatural abilities can mediate with the spiritual world, especially for purposes of healing and divination. These individuals are the shamans, a kind of priest, who are the spiritual leaders of the community. It is believed that all objects have spirits, and that these spirits have human needs and weaknesses. Thus, the trees, the sky, the animals and the dead have spirits which can decide to do good or ill. Their needs have to be taken into consideration to avoid their fury. In a sense, the shamanists are the first 'greens' who preached harmony between human beings and nature. Water, for example, has a soul in the eyes of the shamanists. Cleansing the body or impurities in water is considered an act that would offend the soul of rivers and lakes. Certain shamanists avoid washing their bodies. Only the dead are washed because they are considered to have reached the same stage of spiritual awareness as inert material.

Shamanists believe in a supreme God whom the Turks called *tengri*, which corresponds to the current Turkish word for God, *tanri*. In the tents (*yurt*) of nomad Turks, two fires – one for male ancestors and the other for female ancestors – were kept alive at all times. The hearth (*ocak*) of the family was considered sacred. This belief still lives among Anatolian Turks, where the extinction of a family line, for instance, is metaphorically described by saying 'the family hearth is destroyed'. Believing that certain ocaks or households have healing properties is another practice originating from the shaman period, as are the beliefs relating to Hizir, the shaman god of water, and the practice of divination. Many shamanistic beliefs are still alive in Anatolia (Hassan, 1985).

Shamanists hold that women represent the hidden or unknown elements of cosmic phenomena (*sir*) while men represent the physical or overt (*kut*) aspects. Many authors believe that shamanism originates from the mother cult (Hassan, 1985). Even though shamans generally are male, they often imitate female behaviour and clothing during divinations. In many Turkish tribes in central Asia, women – especially the very young and unmarried or the very old – become shamans. Female shamans are called *utagan*, and the males, *kam*. There are good (white – *ak*) and bad (black – *kara*) shamans. Women can be either. In tribes where woman ancestors were worshipped, the majority of shamans were female. Male shamans had to grow long hair and wear women's clothes, receiving the shaman drum from a woman, before being able to communicate with spirits. One author mentions that there was a tendency to consider women as natural shamans (Mikhailovsky, 1984; Stadling, 1912).

The status of Turkish women during the shamanistic period was more egalitarian. Women certainly had a higher degree of physical mobility, accompanying their men to grazing lands and on war campaigns. In a Chinese document, a tribe of attacking Turkish warriors is described as being accompanied by women on horseback 'with suckling babies wrapped around their breasts' (Avcioglu, 1987). Gender segregation in the Islamic sense did not exist, but polygyny was practised. A wife who gave birth to a son gained the right to rule over her own household and to represent herself until her son reached adult age. There was a hierarchy among the wives. Marco Polo, who visited the court of Kublai Khan during the 1200s, noted that among Tartars, the first wife was always considered the most important; kings were accompanied by their first wives. Motherhood also contributed to the ranking: mothers who bore sons lived in white tents, mothers of daughters in red tents and childless women were given black tents. Married women were considered sacred, with the death penalty levied against those who abducted or raped them.

Turks lived a tribal, nomadic life travelling between grazing lands and plundered settlements to obtain new pastures. In the saga of *Ergenekon*, Turkish mythology suggests that Turks originated from the mating of a wounded warrior with a female wolf. They lived in a narrow valley surrounded by high mountains. When the valley became overpopulated, they lit a great fire and melted the iron ore in one of the mountains, so that tribes could migrate away from the valley in all directions.

Turks came under the influence of Islam during the Arab expansion into central Asia around the tenth century. Those tribes that had become sedentary and established kingdoms were the first to convert. The *Gazne* became the first Turkish–Islamic kingdom when their king, Saltuk Bugra Khan, submitted to Islam in AD 940. The spread of Islam accelerated after the tenth century.

Not all Turks accepted Islam at the same time. Some nomadic tribes preferred to serve the various warring states as hired soldiers at times when they were not tending to their cattle, and to move between countries freely at other times. Those who resisted becoming sedentary also resisted monotheism, much to the annoyance of the believers. One Turkish–Islamic author writing in the tenth century described the nomadic groups: 'These infidels call the earth and sky God. A big tree is God for them. They would worship a wise man as God. May God protect us from their perversions' (Avcioglu, 1987). The author is referring to the shamanic practices retained by the nomads. In time, most of the nomads converted to Islam, but sometimes developed their own heterodox interpretations which, as will be explained later, would find expression in the philosophy of the Anatolian Sufi, Alevi and Bektashi orders.

As more and more nomads became sedentary and accepted Islam, the situation of women deteriorated. Instead of the horse-taming and sword-swinging girl of the steppes, a girl suitable for marriage by the newly converted Turks was then described as 'a girl who has never left her house, who has never been seen or touched by a foreign man, a girl with lower social status than her suitor' (Avcioglu, 1987).

Anatolia

Archaeological discoveries in Anatolia date back some 10,000 years. Among the earliest findings are paleolithic era statuettes of a female idol with a huge abdomen and breasts crouching as if giving birth to a child. Her earliest name is Kabala, which later become Kybele, changing to Artemis in the Hellenistic era, eventually to become the Diana of the Romans. This woman is the Anatolian earth mother, who is the protector of wild animals, hunters and of childbirth and breast feeding. It is believed that the existence of these idols indicates some matriarchal, or at least matrilocal period in the history of Anatolia; but by the time the first written documents occur, at around 2000 BC, patriarchy had already been established.

The first Anatolian written documents are in Assyrian, recording commercial transactions between Anatolians and Assyrians. It is understood from these documents that women had the right to property and to self-representation. They also had the right to negotiate marriage contracts with future husbands. Polygyny was practised (Afetinan, 1982).

The Hittites were an Indo-European people who established the first known Anatolian Empire, which ruled in north-central Anatolia for about 1000 years, flourishing between 1900 BC and 1200 BC, and continuing until 700 BC. They left behind a wealth of cultural documents in cuneiform script. The status of women in Hittite culture was dependent on their reproductive ability. As is still true in rural Anatolia, a woman gained high status as the mother of a son. The king was accompanied by his mother, the *Tavanna*. The king's wife could become queen only after the death of her mother-in-law and only on the condition that she had borne a son.

Hittite laws had some parallels with Islamic laws that were to come 15 centuries later: women were not given the right to self-representation, but were represented by their fathers or husbands; girls could not be married without the permission of their fathers; there was a death penalty for the abduction and rape of young girls. Also similar to Islamic traditions, women had the right to property and employment, but in the case of the Hittites, women received only half the compensation of men (Afetinan, 1982).

The Hittite Empire was followed by the Urartu, the Phrygians and Lydians (about 1200–500 BC). Very little is known about the status of women in these civilizations. Towards the end of the Hittite period, Greeks had begun to invade western Anatolia, entering into long struggles with the resident states (the story of the Trojan war, about 1200 BC, reflects one of these struggles between Greeks and Anatolians). The Aegean region was gradually colonized by the Greeks and incorporated into the Hellenistic world. Greek culture and language spread further in this region after the Roman conquest and constitution of Anatolia as a Roman province in 133 BC.

Christianity began spreading throughout Anatolia soon after its birth. In AD 330, the Roman Emperor Constantine I, who brought Christianity to the Empire, inaugurated an old Greek trading centre as the new city of Constantinople which became the capital city of the eastern Roman, and later the Byzantine, Empire. While the city of Rome in the west fell into decay, Constantinople in the east was to become the spiritual centre of Christianity for some 1000 years. During this latter period, Greek Christian Orthodoxy became established in Anatolia. By the fifth century AD, Anatolia had become entirely Christian.

Turks in Anatolia

> The dust devil dancing on the distant steppes of Turkestan grows into a cyclone as it swirls through Iran and Iraq and bursts on Byzantine Anatolia in the 11th century. (Severy and Stanfield, 1987)

The appearance of Turkish nomads in Anatolia has been recorded in Byzantine documents from the ninth century AD onward. The official date for the Turkish entry into Anatolia is generally given as 1071, when the Byzantine army was defeated by the Seljuks at a battle in Eastern Anatolia. The Seljuks (1077–1308) were Oghuz Turks, a tribe believed to descend from Oghuz Khan, his 6 sons and 24 grandsons. One such tribe, under the leadership of Seljuk Bey, had settled in the area around the northern Caspian Sea during the tenth century. The goal of this kingdom was to expand westward. By 1077, Byzantine rule in most parts of Anatolia was ended, signifying the beginning of the Turkification and Islamization of Anatolia.

The Seljuk kingdom did not last long, gradually decaying into non-existence, as other Turkish tribes continued to migrate into Anatolia, some of which established small princedoms. One of these was the kingdom of the Ottomans (the sons of Osman), who settled in the northwestern corner of Anatolia, adjacent to the Byzantine border. This tribe, which also descended from the Oghuz, was eventually to end the Byzantine presence, unite the various Anatolian kingdoms and extend Turkish presence to the Balkans, Eastern Europe, the Crimea, the Middle East and North Africa. At its height, it controlled an area of 6 million sq. km. and represented the most powerful Sunni-Islamic presence in the world. By the end of the fifteenth century, the Balkan peninsula and Anatolia were under total Ottoman control. The Ottoman expansion towards the northwest during these centuries caused much anxiety in Europe because, among other things, it represented an Islamic threat to Europe. Constantinople was renamed Istanbul and became the capital city of the Ottomans. The Ottoman expansion in the west was to continue, incorporating Greece, Serbia (1521) and Hungary (1526, 1541), only to be halted at the gates of Vienna (1532). In the east, following the incorporation of Syria and Egypt into the empire (1516–17), Ottoman presence extended to Baghdad and Arabia; Ottomans controlled the Balkans and Crimea in the West and their influence in Africa stretched to Algiers. When Egypt was conquered in 1517, the reigning Sultan Selim I (1512–20) took the title of the Caliphate (a caliph was the spiritual and secular leader of Sunni Muslims). After this, the Ottoman dynasty proclaimed that it was the new centre of power representing Islamic unity.

The Ottoman System

The *umma*

People within the Ottoman Empire were not legally identified according to their ethnicity, but rather by their religious faith because Islamic philosophy does not recognize ethnic differences. Only people who share the same religion are considered a nation, which is called an *umma*. People who shared the Muslim faith, regardless of whether they were Turks, Arabs, Kurds or of some other ethnic origin, were considered one nationality: they belonged to the Muslim umma of the Empire. The Empire was not entirely Muslim, of course. The Koran considers only paganism as infidelity. While pagans may not exist in an Islamic state, Christians and Jews must be protected. They are considered 'the people of the book', because each has received the book of God, is mentioned in the Koran and worships the same God. Thus they could exist within a Muslim state and exercise their faith, on the condition that they pay a special tax, the *jizye* (Koran 9:29). Thus, besides the Muslim umma, there were two other nations in the Empire. The 'nation of Christians' included Wallachians, Serbs, Croats, Armenians, Circassians, Greeks and others, and was further divided within itself according to which church they belonged. The 'nation of Jews' consisted mostly of the Jews who left Spain upon King Ferdinand's and Queen Isabella's decree in 1492, and were welcomed to the Empire by Sultan Beyazid II (reign, 1481–1512). Other Jewish groups also existed in the Empire.

Being a Turk in this system did not confer any special privilege. In fact, it could mean hardship. Turks who (together with Greeks and Armenians) constituted the bulk of the peasantry, not only had to pay agricultural taxes but, as Muslims, also had to supply the army with men who disappeared in frequent wars. Furthermore, the central government distrusted the Turkomen, those tribes who still lived as semi-nomads, challenging the central Ottoman despotism and opposing the Sunni religion. The Ottoman dynasty was also fearful that some other aristocracy would capture the throne if any Turkish family were allowed to become strong enough. The Ottoman sultans and their administrators scrupulously distanced themselves from the Turks who were perceived as vulgar people. Refined Ottomans did not speak Turkish, but a mixture of Persian and Arabic, which ordinary people could not understand. In their struggle to prevent common Turks from influencing the central administration, the Ottomans introduced a curious form of slavery which increased the heterogeneity of the population.

The *devshirme* system

A state where everybody was proud of calling himself a slave. A society of slaves in which the slaves were the masters. The highest officials low born. Islam's power wielded by men baptized and raised as Christians. Suleyman's eight grand viziers were all humble born Christians brought to Turkey as slaves. The same went for most top officials and janissaries. (Severy and Stanfield, 1987)

Besides taxation in kind and cash, the Ottomans introduced a new type of tax when they began conquering regions in Europe and Russia. This was sometimes called the 'blood tax'. It was administered between the years 1420–1630. Every few years, an Ottoman committee would set out to visit villages in the colonialized Christian countries to inspect the youth. The committee would select any number of the strongest, most attractive and intelligent boys between 7 and 15 years of age to become slaves of the sultan. The youths would then be taken away from their families as 'blood-tax' and brought to Edirne (Adrianople), where they would submit to Islam and receive diverse schooling in subjects such as physical training, mathematics, religion, Turkish, Arabic and Persian. Those who excelled in sports and martial arts would then be sent to receive further schooling as cadets to become soldiers and officers in the elite Janissary Corps of the Ottoman army. Youths adept in mathematics, languages and other intellectual endeavours would be sent to the palace academy to serve as royal pages, eventually to become the administrators and statesmen of the Empire. This system of slavery was unique because it allowed the slaves to become powerful individuals within the Empire.

The slaves were called *devshirme*, meaning 'to collect'. The devshirme was a perfect system for preventing the formation of an aristocracy which might have threatened the Ottoman dynasty. Youths were not conscripted from Turkish villages as a matter of policy. Non-Turkish boys who had been uprooted from their countries and families had only one loyalty when they became adults – to the sultan and the Ottoman state. The state gave them everything – power and fortune – that their Christian peasant families could never have provided.

It was a system based entirely on merit rather than birthright. Although they were technically slaves, the devshirme eventually commanded so much power serving the sultan that it was considered desirable to be a slave. Women were also conscripted. The wives and mothers of the Ottomans were frequently former non-Muslims. It was common to have female ancestors of Circassian and Georgian stock in many Turkish families. Women from these countries were considered exceptionally beautiful and were brought to the country to become wives or concubines in the harems. The influx of people from so many countries, possessing such varied backgrounds, further contributed to mixing across racial, religious and cultural boundaries which, in turn, created diverse attitudes toward women.

The first three centuries were years of empire building and expansion for the Ottomans: civilization was at its height. The sultans had unchallenged power over large territories on three continents. A skilled and organized bureaucracy secured, for the people of the Empire, justice, relative prosperity and internal peace. Literature, the arts and sciences flourished and the Ottoman armies and fleets threatened the very existence of Christian Europe (Fisher, 1983).

The decay of the Empire is generally accepted as having begun in the seventeenth century with the advent, in the West, of the Renaissance and Reformation, developments in science and technology, the emergence of centralized nation-states with ever-improving military power, the shift of the main international trade routes from the Mediterranean to the open seas and the dawn of Western colonialism, all of which combined to strengthen Europe, while the Ottoman Empire began to stagnate. During the nineteenth century the Ottomans introduced reforms aimed at strengthening the army and the central government to enhance competition with Europe. But provinces were being lost one after the other, while the Empire decayed from within in the hands of corrupt officials and local despots. New ideas of nationalism were sharpening hostilities between the peoples of the Empire. Reforms were often hindered by the Muslim *ulema*, the Islamic theorists, and the janissaries; meanwhile, the European powers were pressing for changes which would guarantee greater foreign financial influence and more liberties for the Christian minorities. The nineteenth century was also a time of almost continuous wars and defeats on many fronts, which demoralized the army. Towards the end of the nineteenth century, the fall of the Empire was imminent. Some of these developments will be explored in more detail in the following section.

Turkish Women During the Ottoman Period

The early centuries (1100–1400)
Women enjoyed greater freedom during the Seljuk and early Ottoman periods than in later times. They participated actively in agriculture and handicraft production and they marketed their produce directly to customers. Royal women often worked in charities, hospitals and religious institutions. In the Turkish tales, *Dede Korkut*, written in the fourteenth century, there are stories in which women are portrayed as free agents riding horses and entering battles.

Marco Polo's eastern counterpart, Ibn Battuta (1308–68), was an Arab who visited Anatolia and other areas inhabited by Turks such as the Crimea, the Caucasus and Central Asia around the 1330s. He gives accounts of the lives of Turkish women. He notes that, unlike other Muslim women of that time,

Turkish women did not veil themselves, could travel long distances unattended by male relatives and were skilled horseback riders. He mentions women working as carpet-weavers, inn-keepers and market-vendors:

> The windows of the tent would be open and their faces visible, for the woman folk of Turks do not veil themselves. One such woman would come to the bazaar in this style, accompanied by her male slaves with sheep and milk, and will sell them for spices. Sometimes one of the women will be in the company of her husband and anyone seeing him would take him to be one of her servants. (Ibn Battuta, 1958)

Ibn Battuta mentions Turkish princes with several wives, each living in their separate residences. But there are no suggestions of veils, gender segregation, harems or eunuchs.

After the fifteenth century

The freedom exercised by women only a few centuries after Turks began converting to Islam struck Ibn Battuta as remarkable. This was gradually to change in the later centuries as the lives of Turkish women increasingly began to be shaped by orthodox Islamic mores, particularly after the sixteenth century when the Ottoman dynasty took the caliphate from Egypt and became the world representative of Sunni Islam. Turkish women progressively lost whatever autonomy and influence they formerly had in public life. Certain practices aimed directly at controlling the autonomy of women.

The harem

The harem system, which signifies strict gender segregation, was introduced in the Ottoman court and among its dignitaries after Istanbul was conquered in 1453 and became the capital of the Empire (Afetinan, 1982). Harem is a derivative of the word *haram*, meaning 'forbidden'. The homes of the Muslim Ottomans were divided into two parts, one of which was known as the harem, the section of the house which was forbidden to all foreigners, particularly foreign men, with the possible exception of male doctors and eunuchs. This section was the domain of the womenfolk – the mother, sisters, wife or wives, female slaves, servants and the children. Only the man of the house and the fathers, sons and brothers of the women could enter a harem. Other men were allowed to enter the other part of the house, the *selamlik*, which means a 'place for greetings'. Most homes had at least one room or a corridor on the first floor of the house functioning as a selamlik. In very poor homes, the selamlik was the garden or the nearest coffee house.

The harem was essentially the private part of the house allocated to family life. It would house bedrooms, living rooms, prayer quarters, the study and other areas for private and recreational use. Harem quarters of the homes of the wealthy were sometimes enormous, consisting of hundreds of rooms. In middle-class families the harem could be a few rooms, usually on the second floor of the house. Lady Montagu, the wife of an eighteenth-century English ambassador, described, in a letter from Edirne (Adrianopole) in 1717, a visit she made to the wife of a high officer. She is greeted at the door of the harem by two black eunuchs who lead her through a gallery between two ranks of good-looking young girls with long, braided hair. She enters a room where the lady of the house, a young woman, is sitting on a low sofa covered with carpets. Her two young daughters are sitting on the floor in front of her and all three of them are wearing clothes richly embroidered in the Turkish style of the time: a shirt, vest, caftan and large trousers, all decorated with jewellery. Lady Montagu is greeted politely and entertained by some dancing and singing. She drinks coffee and is offered marmalade.

There was a hierarchy among the women of the harem, with the mother of the man (the *valide*) at the top, followed by women with sons (the *haseki*), sisters, mothers of daughters, daughters and so on. Each of these women had a number of personal eunuchs and female slaves to serve them. The man of the house did not have access to the sexual favours of the women's personal female slaves, unless the women gave their permission. These personal slaves were often, after some years of service, married off to suitable men to become 'free' wives. The concubines (*odalisk*) were female slaves to which the man had access. Their situation was uncertain; they could become very powerful if they bore sons, or managed to become a favourite sexual partner. It was also possible for them to grow old without ever being noticed; or, worse still, to be disgraced for failure to meet the expectations of the man or the women higher in the harem hierarchy. Life in a harem, despite the luxurious tranquillity it reflected to European visitors, was difficult, laden with intrigue and resentment. Poor families, with homes consisting of only one room, did not have a harem. The harem system reflected the practical implications of gender segregation and relegation of women to the private sphere of life: absolute confinement.

The eunuchs

Because women were considered unable to protect their virtue themselves, it was necessary for men to guard the harem areas against the entrance of unauthorized men. In the homes of wealthy families protection was provided by eunuchs. As was the case with many other customs, the employment of eunuchs first occurred at Topkapi Palace in Istanbul and eventually spread throughout the Empire.

Islam prohibits the castration of Muslims, so eunuchs were non-Muslim slaves brought usually from the Sudan or Ethiopia, but they could be Caucasian or Oriental. Blacks were preferred. During castration, only the testicles were removed. Because the penis was not removed, it was remotely possible for a eunuch to have sexual relations. Black eunuchs were preferred because it was believed that illegitimate offspring could always be detected by skin colour. Black eunuchs were popular status symbols only the very wealthy with large harems could afford. They were expensive and rare because of the low survival rate following the castration operation. An interesting account of the eunuchs at Topkapi Palace is given by a Swedish physician, J. Hedenborg, who visited the Empire in the eighteenth century:

> *Kizlar aga* ['the chief of girls'] is the supervisor of the eunuchs, the unquestionable ruler of the harem and the main protector of the virtues of the princesses. He is the sultan's closest man, has his confidence and often exercises great influence over him. In the absence of higher pleasures, he is only sensitive to gold and power, and sees to it that he is well paid for his services. Usually he is from an Ethiopian tribe, and hence black. But there are exceptions when he may be of another race and colour. The *kizlar aga* uses his personal reputation to influence the sultan over the choice of people for the most important posts; yes, he can even influence the choice of heir to the throne and his fate. They depend on him, both inside and outside the palace. He is also the administrator of the property of the mosques, presides over religious foundations and charities which belong to Mecca and Medina, and holds his own divan once a week to discuss these matters. The chief inspector and his secretary attend the meetings. There are about a total of 400 black eunuchs, who mostly come from Abyssinia (Hedenborg, 1839).

The eunuch phenomenon was a reflection of the general attitude towards women in Muslim society which considered them unable to protect themselves and stay chaste if not guarded by men. In the poorer sections of society, the function of protection and control was fulfilled by the male relatives of the women.

Polygyny

Islamic law allows men to marry up to four women and have sexual relations with their female slaves. This is why the sultan and other wealthy men could have very large harems filled with concubines (the *odalisk*, meaning belonging to the room). With the exception of the sultans and a few other dignitaries whose harems housed hundreds of woman slaves, polygyny was not a major feature of Ottoman Turkish families. There are very few accounts from travellers in Turkish Anatolia which describe polygynous households, even among the wealthiest. The following description is by a German traveller in Anatolia during the sixteenth century:

> Turks rule countries and their wives rule them. Turkish women go around and enjoy themselves much more than any others. Polygamy is absent. They must have tried it but then given up because it leads to much trouble and expense. Divorce is rare, for then the man has to pay in money and goods and daughters are left with the mother (Ortayli, 1985).

There was resistance to polygyny. It was considered decadent, particularly if a first wife had given her husband children. Polygyny was expensive and this could lead to tension in the home. Only the wealthiest – who could pay a bride-price more than once, provide separate residences for each wife and could afford their upkeep – could imagine multiple marriages. Not all wealthy men could practice polygyny: women had the right to negotiate marriage contracts preventing subsequent marriages of their future husbands. They seem to have used this right often. Lady Montagu reflects upon the status of women and polygyny:

> Upon the whole, I look upon Turkish women as the only free people in the empire: the very divan pays a respect to them; and the Grand Signoir himself, when a pasha is executed, never violates the privileges of the harem, which remains unsearched. They are queens of their slaves whom the husband has no permission so much as to look upon, except it be an old woman or two that his lady chooses. 'Tis true their law permits them four wives; but there is no instance of a man of quality that makes use of this liberty, or of a woman of rank who suffers it. When a husband happens to be inconstant (as those things will happen), he keeps his mistress in a house apart and visits her as privately as he can, just as it is with you. Among all the great men here, I only know the *defterdar* [treasurer] that keeps a number of slaves for his own use, and he is spoken of as a libertine, and his wife won't see him, though she continues to live at his house (Montagu, 1898).

Most families were monogamous. This fact is reflected by census figures from the sixteenth century onward, where the avarage Turkish family, both in urban and rural areas, consisted of not more than five or six persons (Ortayli, 1985; Duben, 1985).

The segregated life

How women, so segregated from public life, passed their time in their homes differed according to social class. Women of the upper classes usually received some education during their early years and would learn to read, write and recite the Koran. Before the onset of puberty, around nine or ten years of age, girls would be separated from their brothers to learn womanly arts such as embroidery and playing musical instruments. The few upper-class women who were allowed to have some private education did manage to carry out some intellectual work. A few women became renowned as poets, composers, calligraphers and even one as an astronomer (Taskiran, 1973). In general, however, higher scholarship was deemed unnecessary, even harmful. Girls would be married off within a few years of puberty, after which childbirth and caring for their husbands would become their most important preoccupations. Having as many as 20 children was not unusual although many children died young.

Lady Montagu describes the life of high class women as one of endless leisure, whereby they spent their husbands' money on self-adornment and jewellery and on frequent visits to each other and to the public baths (*hamam*). They also organized picnics, practised embroidery, smoked water pipes, listened to music and prepared exquisite meals. The Turkish culinary tradition, with its rich variety and refined taste combinations, is a reflection of the creative yearnings of these captive women. Johan Hedenborg, in his capacity as a physician, was able to gain some understanding of the lives of the women confined in harems. He provides the following insights, which are less flattering than Lady Montagu's:

> The upbringing of the princesses is not better than that of the princes. But the princes may at least in time be released from their prisons. According to tradition, princesses get engaged to ministers, generals or other high officials when they still are in their cradles. These men are then prohibited from taking other wives or slaves and they become the slaves of their wives rather than their husbands. These relationships which are established for political reasons show many peculiarities. On the one hand a young princess must carry beside her a wrinkled old man as husband, on the other hand the man must love and stay faithful to a woman betrothed to him by the royal highness.
>
> It is said that the lives of the rich and powerful in Turkey, a life without anything to do, is unbearable. In this case the lives of women must be the most unbearable. It would be wrong to think that they have a need to create work the same way as we do; they do not feel such needs, and thus they do not miss them. But the bird in its cage longs after freedom. It is this freedom they can not choose. They are bound to live the same repetitious life within the same circle, most of the time with nothing to do. Their only entertainment is to watch the slaves dance their funny dances, or the shadow theatre and the jugglers, or to spend hours taking baths, or walk a few rounds in the gardens under the shadows of distressing cypress trees, surrounded by high walls. Their lives are narrow, suppressed and monotonous.
>
> The lives of the other Turkish women are much to prefer. The well-off ladies have the right to go on outings, sometimes in their coaches, sometimes on foot, to visit friends or go to the bath-house where they with pleasure spend the whole day in lively discussions. They are accompanied with some slaves or eunuchs. The ladies of the middle class have even more freedom: in groups of five or six, they arrange outings to the country side where they eat their food under the shadow of some old tree or next to a small creek and spend the whole day. Even though they are heavy in body movements, their tongues are exceptionally vigorous.
>
> The poorest women have an almost unlimited freedom; they go everywhere without being noticed, often alone, usually busy with some housekeeping activity, or just entertaining, which consists of going from one place to another either in a coach or on foot. (Hedenborg, 1839)

Lower-class and peasant women generally lacked any kind of an education. However their lives included many productive activities. One of the traditional areas of production, spinning and weaving textiles and carpets, was dominated by women. The other area was agricultural production including food and tobacco growing. Women also worked as laundresses, midwives and street vendors. According to some records, women worked in coal mines as early as the sixteenth century. Some women were engaged in the slave trade (Taskiran, 1973).

The veil

Veiling, which did not exist in Anatolia when Ibn Battuta visited in the mid-fourteenth century, later became compulsory for all Muslim women, particularly in the urban areas of the Empire after the fifteenth century. A mandate for veiling, that is covering the face, is not made in the Koran or in any of the other early texts. The Koran simply prescribes that men and women wear decent clothing which does not reveal the body. The *Hadis*, the volumes describing the example of the Prophet, contains detailed descriptions of which parts of the body women and men may not show to foreigners, members of the opposite sex, close relatives and children, and so on. The Koran stipulates that women are required to cover only their hair and neck and to wear loose clothing. Likewise, men are required to cover their head and all other parts except the areas below the elbows and knees.

Veiling was practised by high class Persian women during the Safavid dynasty in Persia (1499–1736), by Muhammed's widows and by Byzantine princesses. It is believed that the tradition evolved under these influences. The style of clothing and veil differed from one country to another. In Turkey, it consisted of a *yashmak* and *ferajeh*. The ferajeh was a loose-fitting, long coat with long sleeves and a large collar. The yashmak consisted of a thin, white, muslin mouth-piece, which covered the mouth and was tied behind the head, in addition to a large scarf that covered the hair and was tied under the chin, hanging down to the shoulders. In the nineteenth century, the ferajeh and yashmak were replaced by the *charsaf*, meaning 'bed sheet'. That style was inspired by the clothing of women in Egypt, and consisted of a dark coloured cloth hanging from the head to the toes, leaving the face open which, in turn, was covered with a thin, usually black, veil.

Lady Montagu gives an interesting account of the effects of the veil:

> You may guess how effectually this disguises them, so that there is no distinguishing the great lady from the slave. 'Tis impossible for the most jealous husband to know his wife when he meets her.
>
> This perpetual masquerade gives them entire liberty of following their inclinations without danger of discovery. The most usual method of intrigue is to make an appointment to meet the lady at a Jew's shop. The great ladies seldom let their gallants know who they are; and it is so difficult to find it out, that they can very seldom guess at her name they have corresponded with above a half year together. You may easily imagine the number of faithful wives are very small in a country where they have nothing to fear from a lover's indiscretion, since we see so many that have the courage to expose themselves to that in this world, and all the threatened punishment of the next, which is never preached to Turkish damsels. (Montagu, 1898)

In the nineteenth century travelogue of another author, the Italian Edmondo de Amicis, the following comments are made about veiled women:

A foreigner seeing these women with their yashmaks and long gaudy ferajehs might wonder if they were a masked order of nuns, or mad. Because no one is accompanied by a man, one might conclude that all are either widows or unmarried, or the unhappy inhabitants of an enormous convent. For the first few days it is impossible to believe that the Turkish man or woman, who never look at one another, and who pass each other by never being together, can have anything in common at all. Are any Turkish women unfaithful to their husbands? In spite of the jealousy of the husbands, the watchfulness of the eunuchs, the punishment of one hundred lashes pronounced by the Koran to deter sinners, and the sort of insurance company established by Turkish husbands among themselves, the situation here is quite the opposite to that obtaining in other countries. Everything seems to collaborate to damage family happiness. It might even be claimed that the women with yashmaks here commit no less sin than the women without yashmaks in Christian cities. If this was not the case, *Karagöz* [Black eye; a Turkish shadow theatre character] would not mention the word 'cuckold' so frequently. But how is such a thing possible? There are a thousand and one ways. Who watches women separated from their husbands, or not separated but living in a separate house which their husband does not visit each day? Who follows them along the maze of streets or the outer districts? Who prevents the handsome aide-de-camp of the princess doing what I have seen? What about the Christian woman with a veiled friend who welcomes both her and a European man friend into her house on the borders of a Muslim neighbourhood, to assist secret love affairs? Today everything takes place in a most prosaic fashion. The first contact is generally made in the back of shops. It is common knowledge that there are some traders who deal in everything. (Tuglaci, 1984)

Veiling may have helped women to remain anonymous in the streets and aided in a few secret escapades. It is doubtful, however, whether many women dared to attempt such things. An extramarital relationship was considered a great crime for a woman. Adultery was punishable with public whippings and the death penalty. Women were watched continuously.

Women, on the whole, certainly must have resented veiling which was one of the most striking symbols of their captivity. Ottoman history is replete with tragi-comic examples of the struggle women waged against the authorities by continuous attempts to modify their clothing. After each national upheaval, military defeat or on the whim of a sultan, the government would issue a decree, holding responsible the 'immorality' of women, mandating that they cover themselves more. The following are some excerpts from government decrees:

May God protect the spirit of the Ottoman State from all trouble and disaster; it is the land of the righteous and of the learned. Each section of the populace has its own established mode of dress. In spite of this, certain brazen women have begun appearing in the streets dressed in finery, affecting all kinds of innovations in their garments and giving bizarre shapes to their headgear in imitation of shameless women, in order to corrupt the population. Their audacity in lifting the veil of virtue in defiance of decrees to the contrary, their improvisation of modes of dress which violate all notions of honour, have reached such a stage where even women of virtue have begun falling under their influences. These outlandish clothes are prohibited. From now on women may not go out on the streets dressed in ferajeh with wide collars, or swathe their heads with large scarves. The decorative bands on their ferajeh may be no more than one finger's breadth. If any woman is seen out in the streets wearing one of these ferajeh, the collar will be cut there and then in public; and if any person persists in wearing them and offends for a second time, they will be exiled [decree from 1725]. (Tuglaci, 1984)

Women are prohibited from wearing thin veils and must conceal their breasts and hair and refrain from going out in their carriages accompanied by young ornately dressed coachmen.
   Muslim women who use immoral light colour of ferajeh are called upon to change to dark colours within a week. Those who do not obey will be arrested. Tailors who sew light-coloured ferajehs for women will be hanged by the neck in front of their shops. (Tuglaci, 1984; Graham-Brown, 1988)

Such decrees primarily affected urban women. Peasant women were not veiled, not because they were granted more freedom, but simply because the ferajeh and yashmak or the *charsaf* were cumbersome articles which would prevent them from working in the fields. When going to a town, they had to wear a veil. Otherwise they wore the type of clothes many rural women still wear: the baggy trousers (*shalvar*), a blouse and vest, and a head-scarf. However, peasant women, when confronted with a stranger, dropped their eyes and covered their mouth with a piece of their headscarf and turned their back so as not to show their face, reactions that still persist among many rural women in Turkey. The veil symbolized many things which reached beyond being a style of clothing. The following passage, written years later by an Egyptian woman, describes how the veil has affected the psychology of women:

A veil, however high or low, thick or thin . . . remains a veil, with its full meaning until it disappears. It is not just a piece of black or white chiffon, or merely a special type of garment. It is never casually assumed or laid aside without reflection. It presents strange paradoxes. It is a restrictive emphasis on sex relations, and also a moral protection; a sign of utter dependence and also freedom from responsibility; a handicap to real progress and a symbol of special privilege (Woodsmall, 1936).

During the Islamic period, covering the body and hair, if not the face, was also practised by Christian, Jewish and Alevi women in the Empire.

Other prohibitions

From the fifteenth century onward, the status of Turkish women became quite similar to that of women in other Muslim societies. Restrictions were characterized by a vertical division of society on the basis of gender. Women were confined to the home and family. Men took care of public affairs, in accordance with the Islamic law, the *Sheriat*. Besides gender segregation, restrictions took in many other areas which effectively isolated women, allowing them almost no autonomy.

The physical movement of women was restricted by a variety of prohibitions. A Muslim woman was not allowed to travel long distances (defined as more than 90 km.) unless accompanied by a male relative. Short-distance movements were also restricted: Muslim women could not walk in the streets accompanied by a man, even their husband, because it was believed that this might stir the imagination of other men. Neither could they appear unchaperoned. A woman walking alone on the street would be suspected of seeking illicit adventure and could be reproached by any man and interrogated as to where she was going, why, etc. 'Honourable' women had to be accompanied by other women, eunuchs, servants or children during any excursion outside the home.

Women were forbidden by law from taking boat excursions with men (decree from 1610); from entering shops which sold cream and sweets (1603); from sitting at outdoor cafés; from entering the inner parts of shops where they could not be observed from the street. Women could not go out from their homes more than four times a week (1754); could not go out on days when the sultan would be visiting (1757); could not go out after the evening prayer, could not enter certain districts of towns. They had to sit in places allocated to women in public transport, restaurants, mosques and all other public places. They could not take boats or ride trams for entertainment; women were to disembark at the exact place of destination and were forbidden to take the same vehicle twice on the same day – this to keep them from touring the town just for fun. Women could not loiter in the streets, gaze at other people, make gestures to or mimic others. They could not even look out of the windows of their homes unless the windows were barred with special shutters.

Women were not allowed to carry out important public functions, whether in government or religion. In the religious hierarchy, women could become, at most, a *hafiz*, a person who could recite the Koran. They could not lead congregations. The only public function they could perform was charity work. In a court of law the testimony of two women was considered equal to that of one man. Even though women could own property, their options for directly participating in commerce and production were extremely limited. They had to employ a male servant or relative to manage their holdings. Direct participation in such activities was easier for rural women, but nearly all rural families were so poor that most women had no holdings to administer.

Women could not inherit agricultural land and they inherited only one-half the property inherited by their brothers and sons. They were often not given the bride price, to which they were entitled, at the time of their marriage. In spite of the fact that some women did pursue careers outside their homes, they did so under duress because 'honourable' women were not supposed to leave their homes for that purpose. Normally a man would not allow his wife to work outside the family unless he was forced to do so by extreme financial hardship. In addition to her husband, a woman's other male relatives would attempt to dissuade her from such 'shameful' behaviour. If a woman were successful in combating all of the men opposed to her interests outside the traditional responsibilities of a wife and mother, she still could not escape the regulation of her enterprise by male relatives. Women very rarely owned their own tools of production. In addition, they normally negotiated their financial compensation from an extremely disadvantageous position. They were, in the minds of men, after all, violating societal standards by pursuing such endeavours. Thus most peasant and urban women were very poor.

Women's opportunities for intellectual enhancement were extremely limited. Girls could go to primary school between the ages of five and nine, learning to read, write and memorize the Koran, but even this was deemed unnecessary for the majority of women. Further education was discouraged and even considered harmful. Only the daughters of high-class liberal families could receive private further education.

Girls were under the protection of their fathers and other male kin until they were married, at which time the responsibility was assumed by their husbands. Women very often were given away in marriage by their families to a man whom they had never seen or with whom they had never spoken. Premarital friendship with the opposite sex was unthinkable. Except for daughters in powerful families, women could not negotiate, with their future husbands, a marriage contract which would protect their interests.

Within marriage a woman was, by law, obligated to obey and serve her husband and could be physically punished by him for infractions. Polygyny and effortless divorce were the prerogatives of men. In divorce, a man did not need to take his case to a court. It was enough for him, in front of witnesses, to repudiate his wife by simply pronouncing the words 'I divorce thee' three times. He did not have to give an explanation for divorcing his wife. A woman, on the other hand, could get a divorce only in extreme cases, when her husband did not provide for the family or if he was impotent, and then she had to prove her case in a court of law. A divorced woman could not have permanent custody of her children, but had to leave the boys when they were six years old and the girls when they were nine, with her ex-husband's family. A divorced or widowed woman would have to return to her parental home or, if she was older, she had to live with her sons. A Muslim woman living alone was extremely unusual and prompted suspicion about her morality, particularly if she was young.

How did women feel? Did they yearn for more freedom? Did they accept their situation with resignation or take it for granted without question? Did they ever wish to rebel? It is, unfortunately, difficult to find documents which reveal how Turkish women felt during this period. Illiterate, isolated from public life and led to believe they were insignificant, women did not, apparently, think it worthwhile to ponder their destiny and record their thoughts and feelings. However, they seem to have been quite rebellious. The writer, Edmondo do Amici, describes his observations in this respect:

> They are mocking and disrespectful. It has been known for a European man who understands Turkish to hear an elegant woman speak words of such indelicacy, that in our countries only women of the lowest class could be heard to use them. The resentment they feel inside increases as they meet more European women, and their knowledge of our customs incites them to rebel.
>
> When rebellions occur here women are in the forefront. They gather together, armed with weapons, stop the carriages in which the viziers are hiding, pour streams of abuse at them, attack with stones in their hand, and resist the use of force. (Tuglaci, 1984)

Restructuring of Empire (*Tanzimat*)

By the nineteenth century, Europe had surpassed the Ottomans in commerce, technology, science, military power and political influence – a fact that made itself very painfully felt in the many military defeats, loss of colonies and economic crises within the Empire. Modernization was necessary and, for the Ottoman intellectuals of the time, this meant an imitation of Europe. Towards the end of the eighteenth century, the need for reformation had led the Ottoman administrators to send scholars to Europe and bring foreign experts to the Empire. The increased cultural and technical exchange resulted in an Ottoman intelligentsia, which had become acquainted with Western thought, and emerged to form an alternative to the monopoly of the Sunni-Islamic orthodoxy in the country.

In the first half of the nineteenth century there were a series of reforms, beginning with the abolition of the Janissary Corps in 1826 with a massacre (by then the janissaries had become a corrupt assortment of rioters). A new army was established, together with other military reforms. The zeal for reformation culminated in the announcement of the Gulhane Royal Edict of 1839 which promised civil freedoms and a certain amount of liberalization. The period 1839–1878 is known as Tanzimat, or the period of restructuring. This period constitutes the beginning of change in Turkey. In addition to the army, government institutions and public services were reorganized. New high schools and technical universities, many staffed by Europeans, were established. Western language education was introduced, Western literature was translated, the Turkish novel was born and newspapers and magazines flourished. For the first time in the Empire's history, Ottoman printing presses began introducing new ideas, waging debates on social and political questions and following developments in Europe.

For some, the Tanzimat was a period of enlightenment. For others, it began the capitulation to Western political, economic and cultural values. Most reformers were upper class, educated elites, who wanted, superficially, to imitate the West, eclectically taking from it technology, knowledge, lifestyles and so forth. They had little appreciation of the underlying historical processes which led to Western political and economic superiority. The advances in Western industrialism and technology had left the Ottoman Empire in such a disadvantaged position that no amount of imitation could bridge the economic gap. As Western products poured into the country, all attempts at independent industrial development failed and the Ottoman Empire became increasingly dependent on the West.

This negatively affected the lives of the populace who began to resent the changes. Supported by religious leaders and theologians, whose position was compromised by the attempted reforms, people blamed the deterioration in their living standards on the new wave of Westernization and the abandonment of basic Islamic values. It was at this time that the tug of war began between people who may be roughly grouped as the 'Westernists' (also sometimes called 'progressives' or 'democrats') and the 'Islamists' (also called 'fundamentalists'). This struggle continues today in Turkey and still colours the ideological/political debate in many other Muslim countries.

In general, the affluent, educated upper classes supported Westernization because they had much to gain in positions of power in a state which could be made to collaborate with the West. The lower classes, on the other hand, particularly the small business owners and the peasantry whose interests were threatened by the advancement of Western capitalism, yearned for the traditional lifestyles. They sought their salvation in religion. In the ideological struggle between the Westernists and Islamists, the status of Muslim women, that symbol of Islamic dogma, was to become a burning issue.

The Debate on the Turkish Family

One of the main themes in the social debate waged in the press during this period was the crisis at the foundation of Ottoman society, the Turkish family. This unit, it was said, had so degenerated that the effort to build a stronger society had to begin there. The Turkish family could not be strengthened as long as women were repressed and kept ignorant. Both the press and Turkish novels, which began to appear about this time, were critical of practices such as polygyny, forced early marriage and limited education for women.

Women's lack of education was particularly deplored. The ignorance in which women were kept was seen as both the reason for, and result of, their repression. How could the young men, the daughters and mothers of future Ottoman society be enabled to build stable, enlightened families, it was argued, if they continued to be raised by ignorant mothers? How could the Ottoman male, burdened as he was with the struggle to earn a living and build a better society, find strength and inspiration in his family when, at the end of a burdensome work day, he had nothing to look forward to but the companionship of a primitive, captive creature who was unable to understand any of his endeavours? (Taskiran, 1973; Caporal, 1982)

These arguments were not feminist, but waged by self-serving men who showed little empathy with the deep humiliation experienced by women. There was little criticism of practices such as veiling, gender segregation or of the deep suspicion and misogyny underlying all the restrictions on women. That women should be considered equal to men was not mentioned at all. These debates were opportunistic in that men wanted women to receive some education in order to save men and the society they had built. They wanted education for women, so that they might become better wives, companions and mothers, in the service of men:

> Women should be educated in the same way as men with a view toward enabling them to help and comfort their husbands, on whose shoulders rests the responsibility of earning a living for their families. Moreover, education will greatly help women towards a better understanding of religious and secular considerations and encourage them *to obey their husbands, to refrain from going against their wishes, and above all, to protect their honour* [my emphasis – T.K.]. (Graham-Brown, 1988)

Calling for the right to education for women was in itself, however, a positive development. After seeing how learning to read and write changed her two grand-daughters, an older woman asked one of them to write the following sentences which were published in a newspaper: 'When I was young, men considered it shameful for women to know how to read and write. Now I realize that this was in order to keep us women on the same level as animals' (Taskiran, 1973).

The Beginnings of Emancipation

Thus the first reforms to women's rights occurred in education. In 1842, a school for midwives was opened in Istanbul. This was followed by the establishment of the first junior high school for girls in 1858 and a technical school in 1869. The most important breakthrough was the founding of a teachers' college for girls in 1870. Such an institution was necessary to provide girls' schools with female teachers, but it also signified the beginning of the instruction of girls outside traditional areas. In teachers' colleges, instead of learning sewing and child care, girls were taught how to teach others to read and write, geography and history. Teachers' colleges were later established in many other provinces.

There were some peculiarities in the quality of the education girls were receiving. For instance, literacy was not a requirement for girls admitted to the school of midwives, and practical training was not allowed: they received instruction on how to help women give birth by practising with mannequins. Gender segregation was carefully maintained. When no female teachers were available, only old, handicapped or unattractive male teachers were selected for leading classes. Male and female instructors had to sit in different rooms. Men could enter these schools only with written permission from the Ministry of Education (Taskiran, 1973).

The opening of schools for girls did not lead to a boom in women's education. People were generally suspicious of education for girls. Only the daughters of progressive families would participate. In 1873, 31 years after the first girls' school was opened, there were only 294 women in the country with graduation certificates. In addition, upper-class Muslim women were sent to private foreign schools, or received private tutoring, so the total number of educated women was somewhat higher than this (Taskiran, 1973).

Two other reforms which favoured women were carried out during this period. One gave women the right to inherit agricultural land. This greatly advanced the prospects of peasant women, even though they were allowed to inherit only half the land allotted to male heirs. Female slavery was also abolished, putting an end to the notorious practice of keeping *odalisks*.

Despotism

The Empire's first constitution was promulgated in 1876 but was suspended by Abdulhamid II only two months after its adoption. Later, when this Sultan was defeated in battle by the Russian Army, he blamed the defeat on the Empire 'falling into decadent cosmopolitanism with the degeneration of national traditions and morals'. By his order, all reforms were halted. Liberals and other democrats went into exile or hiding within the Empire. The opposition were called the Young Turks. A new period of despotism began which was to last for 30 years.

Liberal ideas continued to spread, however, both because of the activities of the Young Turks living in exile and because, despite severe censorship, the country experienced a new wave of publication of books and periodicals. The debate on the status of women continued. The first periodical for women, *Hanimlara Mahsus Gazete* (Gazette for Ladies), with an all-woman staff, began publication in this period. It was edited by Fatma Aliye, one of the first Turkish feminists, who waged an effective polemical war against the repression of women. She was the first Muslim woman to write a book on women in Islam that stirred great interest. It was translated into several languages, including Arabic and French (Taskiran, 1973).

No new reforms were introduced during the Abdulhamid despotism; however ideas were ripening and lifestyles were changing. It is during this time that two distinct types of harems emerged: one styled by Western influence and the other by Islamic custom, as entertainingly described by Edmondo de Amicis (1864–1908):

The harem of the young, unprejudiced Turkish man, who supports his wife's European ideas and the harem of the bigoted man, influenced by his elderly mother, who domineers in the house, is a strict Muslim and hostile to innovation. The first resembles the house of a European gentlewoman. It contains a piano, which the mistress of the house is taught to play by a Christian piano instructor. The rooms contain sewing boxes, small wickerwork chairs, a *chaise longue* and a desk. There is a portrait of the master of the house executed in charcoal by an Italian artist living in Pera [a district in Istanbul] on the wall; in one corner is a bookshelf with twenty or so volumes, among them being a Turkish–French dictionary and the most recent issues of an illustrated fashion magazine lent by the wife of the Spanish consul. The mistress enjoys painting pictures of flowers and fruit. She tells her female friends that she is never bored. In her spare time she keeps a diary. At a set time of the day she receives her French tutor, who, naturally is a humpbacked and wheezy old man, and does her best to converse with him. Occasionally a German woman photographer from Galata [a district in Istanbul] comes to take pictures. When she is ill she is examined by a European physician, who may even be young and handsome, because her husband is not stupidly jealous like his old-fashioned friends. Occasionally a French dressmaker comes for a fitting of a dress, cut according to the illustrations in the fashion magazine; and the wife surprises her husband in this dress on a Thursday night, the sacred night of Muslim husbands and wives, and the night when the master will pay a nocturnal visit to his 'rose petal'. Her husband, who occupies an important position, promises to let her have a glimpse through the open doors of the first large ball of the season held at the British Embassy. This woman is a European whose religion happens to be Islam, and she is happy to tell her friends that her life resembles that of a Christian woman. Even if her woman friends and relatives do not lead a similar life, they can at least speak openly about the same subjects, chattering about fashion and the theatre and making fun of 'ignorant ideas, fanatic piety and superstition', that 'the time has come to live in a more rational manner'.

What about the other harem? Everything there is entirely Turkish, from the clothing of the mistress down to the smallest utensils and articles. No book but the Koran enters these houses and no newspaper but the *Istanbul Gazette* is bought. When the mistress falls ill, the doctor is not called; instead a spiritual healing woman is called, who is believed to possess supernatural power to cure all ills. If the bride's mother and father have been infected with Europeanism, they are permitted to visit their daughter only once a week. All the entrances to the house are tightly barred and bolted. Even if the mistress was unfortunate enough to have learned a little French in her childhood, nothing else but the European air she breathes is European here. Her mother-in-law may thrust the worst kind of European novel into her hands and then demand with sarcasm, 'Do you see what that wonderful society you wish to emulate, really is? What moral women it produces? What a fine example it sets for you?' (Tuglaci, 1984)

Renewed Optimism and New Reforms

In 1908, under army threat, Abdulhamid II was forced to declare a second constitutional period. The political party, the Ittihat ve Terakki (Unity and Progress), established in exile by the Young Turk movement, came into power. The monarch's privileges were restricted, elections were held and a new parliament with two chambers was established.

An episode from this period illustrates, once again, the deep pain and humiliation women experienced. It describes the dismantling of Sultan Abdulhamid II's harem following his deposition in 1909, in accordance with the law prohibiting female slavery:

> One of the most mournful processions of the many mournful processions of fallen grandeur that passed through the streets during these days was one composed of the ladies of the ex-Sultan's harem on their way from Yildiz to the Topkapi Palace. These unfortunate ladies were of all ages between fifteen and fifty and so numerous that it took thirty-one carriages to convey them. They were collected in the Topkapi Palace in connection with one of the strangest ceremonies that ever took place there. It is well-known that most of the ladies of the harems of Turkish sultans were Circassians, the Circassian girls being very much esteemed on account of their beauty and consequently very expensive. . . . The Turkish government telegraphed to the different Circassian villages in Anatolia, notifying them that every family which happened to have any of its female members in the ex-Sultan's harem [was] at liberty to take them home, no matter whether the girls had been originally sold by their families or had been taken by force.
>
> In consequence of this, a large number of Circassian mountain-men came in their picturesque garb into Istanbul, and on a certain fixed day they were conducted in a body to the Old Palace of Topkapi, where, in the presence of a Commission, they were ushered into a long hall filled with the ex-Sultan's concubines . . . all of whom were then allowed to unveil themselves for the occasion. (Ahmed, 1982)

By this time, at least three ideological perspectives had crystallized on how the status of women could be improved.

The first position was that of the Westernists, many of whom were staunch critics of the decadence of the monarchy and the domination of religion over society. Most of these people sympathized with or supported the Young Turks. They maintained that the Empire had to be secularized, and all prohibitions against women suspended. Some Westernists demanded complete equality for women in all spheres of life. One author from this group, Semseddin Sami (1850–1904), in 1880 wrote a book about women in which he developed quite advanced egalitarian ideas. The most famous personage from that era was the humanist male poet, Tevfik Fikret (1867–1915), a renowned atheist, two of whose phrases became feminist slogans: 'when women are degraded, humanity is debased' and 'a nation which does not educate its daughters condemns its sons to spiritual desolation.' There were also Islamic Westernists, who called for religious reform, criticizing the *ulema* (theologians) for distorting Islam.

The Islamists took the opposite position. According to them, the degeneration of the Empire and its institutions was a result of the betrayal of basic Islamic principles. They called for a return to traditional practice with a rigid application of Islamic law. This group opposed all public appearances of women, maintaining that their place was in the privacy of their homes, confined to their duties as wives and mothers. The Islamists saw the 'emancipation' exercised by women, who had begun wearing thin veils and sometimes dared to walk in the streets together with men, as proof that the moral values and the future of the country were in danger. One of the foremost figures of this movement, the poet Mehmet Akif (1873–1936), maintained that Islam had given women all the freedoms they needed and declared the whole movement for women's rights was an imperialistic conspiracy to destroy the morals of the Empire. Another Islamist, Sait Halim Pasha (1863–1921), wrote a book in which he attempted to prove, from an historical perspective, that all civilizations where women had public roles had sooner or later been destroyed. Islamists justified all prohibitions on women: the veil, gender segregation and curfew were all necessary to protect women from immoral assaults. Polygyny was necessary to stop adultery and prostitution; it also benefited women by providing them with new aids to help with the housework. Surprisingly, Islamists agreed that women needed more formal education so that they might become better mothers, wives and Muslims. However, they were opposed to instruction in sciences (such knowledge might endanger women's health because it would excite and confuse their weak minds); history and politics (which might lead them to revolt); foreign languages (which might give them inappropriate ideas); and music (which could awaken erotic yearnings and lead to adultery).

The third perspective was that of the 'Turcophiles'. The nineteenth century was a period of national awakening and the breakdown of the *umma* system in the Empire. As the different national and ethnic minority groups began to revolt against Ottoman rule with nationalistic demands, and as the size of the Empire shrank with each successful uprising, a new consciousness began to surface among Turkish-speaking Ottomans. The Turcophiles began to define themselves in ethnic terms rather than as Muslims, and looked to Asia and the pre-Islamic epoch for inspiration about how a future society organized along national lines might best reflect the true ethnic character of the Turks. While Westernists turned to Europe and Islamists turned to Arabia for inspiration, the Turcophiles turned to Asia and imagined a society based on the egalitarian ethics of pre-Islamic Turkish civilizations. They envisioned a society where men and women would have equal rights in all spheres in life. The ideological founder of this movement, a man named Ziya Gökalp (1876–1924), said: 'In the future, Turkish ethics must be founded on democracy and feminism' (Taskiran, 1973). However, the theories on which the Turcophiles based their arguments were as vague as their actual knowledge of pre-Islamic Turkish communities. Not only did they describe the new society in excessively utopian terms, but their ideology also carried seeds that might lead to a racist megalomaniacal pan-Turkism – the ideal of uniting all Turks in the world into one nation. On the whole, however, the Turcophiles made positive contributions towards the goal of women's emancipation with their nationalistic agitation for an egalitarian society. One of the foremost agitators in this movement was a woman, Halide Edip (1884–1964), who later became one of the heroines of the struggle for national independence.

In 1911, the first girls' high school (in preparation for university studies) was opened. Junior high schools for girls were established in many Anatolian provinces. In 1914, Istanbul University began presenting single lectures for women and in 1920 women were allowed to enrol for entire courses at the University. In 1921, a few mixed classes, with women sitting in one section and men in another, were being held. Women entered classes veiled, lifted them during the lecture and lowered them afterwards. In 1923, all gender segregation was ended. Four women received law certificates from Istanbul University in 1924. The first six woman doctors graduated from the school of medicine in 1927 (Taskiran, 1973; Woodsmall, 1936).

The Family Code was revised in 1917, in an attempt to limit polygyny. Men were required to obtain written permission from their first wives in order to be allowed to marry a second. From 1908 to 1921, women were much more active in public life. Many women's organizations were started, particularly for charitable purposes. More importantly, Turkish women, for the first time in Ottoman history, began to take up jobs outside their homes in massive numbers. These were years of worldwide war and humiliating defeat on many fronts. Women's labour was necessary for wartime production. Women in the cities began working in clerical jobs, factories and hospitals. In rural areas women often took over the task of transporting food to the battle lines and to civilians in the cities.

Even if their participation in outside jobs was necessary, the presence of women in public life caused anger and they were frequently assaulted, beaten and sometimes raped. The governor of Kastamonu, a northern province, prohibited all women from going out of their homes. In Izmir, women going to a theatre were prevented from entering and beaten by a mob. In Istanbul, a 'People's house', where the Turcophiles held lectures for mixed audiences, was stormed by the Islamists, who condemned the meetings as being immoral because 'women were being corrupted and incited to revolt by reciting poetry and playing violins' (Taskiran, 1973).

The Fall of the Empire and the Formation of the Republic

In 1908, the Young Turks succeeded in reinstating the constitution and a second period of parliamentary government and reform was launched. Democratic government had many foes, however: the major European powers and Russia did not want a resurgence of the Ottoman Empire; various ethnic groups within the Empire were pressing for independence; and reactionary forces inspired by the Sultan battled to retain their power. The Young Turks failed to initiate all of the promised reforms and within a relatively short time degenerated into a military dictatorship.

Austria annexed Bosnia-Herzegovina and Bulgaria secured complete independence in late 1908. During the following years, the government had to subdue several internal insurrections. In 1911, Italy attacked the Ottoman provinces in North Africa, which resulted in their loss. The two Balkan wars waged during the next two years resulted in the termination of Ottoman control in the entire Balkan region. Russia was threatening the Eastern borders. The fall of the Empire was imminent.

The Germans had been providing military assistance to the Ottoman army, at the request of the sultan, for more than a decade. During the months preceding the outbreak of World War I, the Young Turks sought assurances from the major European powers that the remaining Ottoman territories would not be overrun by Russian troops. Failing to gain such assurances from Great Britain or France, the Young Turks were forced to repay their debt to Germany. Warships under the command of the Young Turk government pre-emptively opened fire on several Russian Black Sea port cities. This was the beginning of the final phase of the fall of the Ottoman Empire.

The exhaustion brought about by the wars and skirmishes fought in the years prior to World War I left the Turkish military forces in a weakened condition. Fifty-two divisions of Turkish soldiers fought valiantly, however, and made a noteworthy contribution to the Central Powers in battles on the eastern front. The successful defensive waged by Turkish troops against Allied forces on the Gallipoli Peninsula overlooking the Dardanelles Strait, the seaway to Istanbul and the Black Sea, went down in history as one of the most violent battles of World War I.

The Turkish ability to resist was eventually exhausted and the government was forced to sign a humiliating cease-fire agreement two weeks prior to the cessation of hostilities on the Western front on 11 November 1918. The Mundros armistice allowed for Allied occupation of Anatolia. Istanbul was occupied by British, French and Italian troops. Izmir and the surrounding area was occupied by Greek forces which immediately began expanding into the east and north. They claimed all western Anatolia including Istanbul. The 1920 Treaty of Sèvres was severe: the state of Turkey was to be reduced to northern Anatolia and Istanbul. Autonomous Kurdish and Armenian states were to be created. Italy and France were to share areas of occupation in southern Anatolia. All Turkish claims to external lands were annulled: the Arab provinces were to be divided among Great Britain, France and Italy. The dispossession of areas outside the Turkish homeland was not contested, but Turks were strongly opposed to the other terms of the treaties. The preservation of the Empire was no longer an issue: it was considered lost. Now the motherland and the very existence of the Turks were being threatened. But the dismemberment of Turkey did not occur because, as the diplomats negotiated, the Turkish struggle for independence was being organized under the leadership of a military commander, Mustafa Kemal.

The national struggle for independence and women's rights
In 1919, Mustafa Kemal was assigned to Anatolia to supervise the demobilization of the Ottoman troops and disposition of supplies. Upon landing in Samsun, a city on the Black Sea coast, Kemal instead began organizing the resistance movement, which eventually led to the Turkish war of independence, the abolition of the monarchy, the declaration of the Republic, and the abolition of the Caliphate and Islamic law. There followed a programme of very ambitious reforms, designed to change the face of the country, which has been described by a prominent historian as 'perhaps the most revolutionary programme accomplished with such systematic awareness within such a short period of time in any country at any time in history' (Toynbee, 1964).

Mustafa Kemal is now well-known, as is the national struggle for independence and the contribution women made to it at all levels of society. Women became highly visible, contributing to the struggle not only as suppliers of food and arms to the front, but also as soldiers, commanders of troops and political agitators (Afetinan 1982; Taskiran, 1973). In Ankara, the capital, there is now a statue of a peasant woman who symbolizes Turkey's liberation: her head is covered with a scarf, she is wearing a shalvar and is leaning forward slightly under the weight of a cannon-ball which she is carrying to the battle front. The self-sacrificing contributions women made to the struggle were later exploited by Kemalists working to bring women equal legal rights.

The struggle for independence was supported by almost all levels of Turkish society, including the Westernists, Islamists and Turcophiles. During those early years, there was no mention of women's rights: the nationalists did not want to lose the support they had from religious leaders who had great influence over ordinary citizens. Most men were grateful for the contribution women were making, but there was a tacit assumption that women would return to their homes when the struggle was over.

The Republic and Kemalism
Once the Republic was established and Mustafa Kemal (Atatürk) became its first president in 1923, he hinted that changes were to come. The only documents we have from Atatürk that illuminate his thoughts are a collection of speeches – he was more of a pragmatist than an ideologist. There were three foundations to his philosophy (popularly termed 'Kemalism'): nationalism, secularization and Westernization. He believed in giving Turks an ethnic identity independent of their umma position. As mentioned, Ottomans did not acknowledge ethnicity. All Muslims – Kurds, Arabs, Turks, or any other groups – belonged to the same nation of Muslims – the umma. A new national consciousness was developing among Turkish-speaking peoples of the Empire during the nineteenth century. After the founding of the Republic, the ethnic characteristic was to be emphasized.

The second Kemalist principle, secularization, was essential in the redefinition of Turks in nationalistic terms. Islam, with its umma thinking, had taken from Turks their ethnic identity. In order to establish national unity within the Republic, religion had to be de-emphasized. Secularization was necessary in order to realize the third principle of Kemalism, Westernization. The West, for Kemalists, represented the height of contemporary civilization: Turks should adopt elements of this civilization without compromising their Eastern identity. The essential characteristics of Western civilization were to be incorporated into the Turkish system in a positive, pragmatic way. Neither Westernization nor a redefinition of the national identity as originating from old Turkish civilizations was possible within the framework of Islamic law.

Thus, after the Republic was proclaimed, a programme was initiated to realize the positivistic philosophy of Kemalism. Once again, the status of women as symbols of Islamic fundamentalism became one of the most important issues. Atatürk prepared people for the changes in his many speeches:

A society which satisfies itself with only one-half of its population enjoying contemporary rights and responsibilities paralyses its other half. Life is activity. If only one-half of a society is active and the other half is forced into idleness, that society becomes paralysed. It cannot function. If our society needs science and technology, both our men and our women, equally, must master these.

It is in the arms of our mothers that we learn about life. Our nation is determined to be strong. One of our greatest needs today is to give the Turkish mother the status she deserves. Our women are also going to master the sciences and be educated equally at every level as men. Women and men are going to work side-by-side in serving society.

I see women who, as soon as they see a man, hide their heads and faces with some cloth, kneel by the sidewalk and turn their backs, as if they must hide, disappear from the sight of men. Gentlemen! What is this! Is this how the mothers, the daughters of a civilized nation should behave? (Taskiran, 1973)

Reforms scorecard

Soon after the Republic was established, a commission was formed to revise and reform the Islamic Family Code in collaboration with the theologians. This effort received much criticism in parliament. Kemalists were critical that the commission was not ready for radical reform on the status of women, while religious groups were worried that women might receive too many rights. The commission appeared to make no progress. Proposed reforms, such as raising the age of marriage to nine for girls and ten for boys, were insignificant. Each development which implied a liberalization of gender segregation met fierce resistance in parliament. For instance, a police officer who had allowed women to sit beside their husbands in buses was severely criticized when the case was brought to parliament. Whether unmarried girls should be allowed to be examined by doctors in a national venereal disease prevention programme was endlessly discussed and then prohibited on moral grounds. Proposals for women to be counted as citizens in the national census and given the right to vote were turned down (Taskiran, 1973). No advance was made either in the

Family Code, or in any other area that needed reform.

The monarchy had been abolished in 1922, but one of the Sultan's cousins was still representing the Caliphate in Istanbul. This implied that the Republic of Turkey was still an Islamic religious state. The Caliph enjoyed influence with the masses, and sometimes challenged the republican government by behaving as if he were the monarch. In a sudden, unexpected decision, typical of Atatürk's pragmatism, the position of the Caliphate was abolished on 3 March 1924. This was an extremely bold decision: Turkey was declaring to the Sunni-Muslim world that it had ceased to honour their spiritual leader. The Caliph was asked to leave the country. The paragraph in the constitution which stated that the state religion of Turkey was Islam was changed to 'The Republic of Turkey is a secular state.' The hegemony of Sunni orthodox theocracy in Turkey was broken and the road to secularization was opened (Kongar, 1979).

These incidents led to the first resistance against Kemalism. Some dissident Islamist parliament members were scandalized and resigned in protest. A political party was formed, including liberals, fundamentalists and other groups opposed to the Kemalists. A group lead by a sheik in eastern Anatolia revolted against the government, demanding, among other things, an immediate return to Islamic order. The Kemalist government imposed martial law in 1925. All opposition to the government and any criticism of the reforms to come were to be considered acts of treason against the state. Special courts (Independence Tribunals) to handle these violations were established. All opposition was effectively suppressed.

Soon after the declaration of martial law, the commission which had been working to reform the Islamic Family Code was suspended. A new commission was assigned to translate the Swiss Civil Code. On 17 February 1926 this Code was presented to parliament. Any discussion or criticism of the Code was prohibited and the translated Swiss Civil Code was ratified to replace the Family Code.

Overnight, Turkish women had gained exactly the same civil rights as those of women in Switzerland! Polygyny was abolished and women were given equal rights in matters relating to marriage, divorce, inheritance, representation, testimony and custody of children. The minimum age for marriage was raised to eighteen. Mutual consent at marriage became compulsory. Criticism of the new Code was prohibited. One newspaper published a cartoon depicting the new 'emancipated' Turkish woman stepping onto the dirigible of 'liberation' and releasing weights of honour, shame and virtue, in order to lift-off. The owner, the editor and the cartoonist were arrested on charges of inciting revolt (Caporal, 1982).

Other reforms followed: all educational facilities were opened to women; wearing Western-style clothing was allowed; the veil, though not prohibited, was no longer compulsory. Atatürk urged women to unveil: 'Uncover your faces and look the world in the face' (Woodsmall, 1936). Elite urban women were soon wearing the latest Paris-inspired, two-piece suits and hats. The Islamic calendar and Arabic script were replaced with the Gregorian calendar and a Latin alphabet. Ottoman and Arabic titles were abolished and replaced by Western-style surnames: Mustafa Kemal adopted the surname Atatürk – 'father of Turks'. Research institutions for Turkish history and language were established. Organizations promoting religious and class domination were prohibited (the Kemalists opposed Communism as well as religious rule). In 1927, the Istanbul Women's Alliance (no doubt upon Atatürk's encouragement: he had begun giving speeches on the desirability of women's political participation) consented to add the struggle for female suffrage to its programme.

In 1930, a second attempt at democracy was made: martial law was lifted. Another political party consisting of liberal as well as religious and monarchist opposition surfaced. A new riot broke out, this time in western Anatolia, demanding the reinstitution of Islamic law. Martial law was proclaimed once again. It was to continue until 1949.

Women were given the right to participate in municipal elections in 1930, and the right to vote for and be elected to parliament in 1934. Thus Turkish women gained political rights before many women in Western countries. Suffrage was granted to women in France in 1945, Italy in 1945, Belgium in 1948 and Switzerland in 1971 (Abadan-Unat, 1986). Since then, women in Turkey have, by law, had equal rights with men.

The Republican reforms reflected the ambitions of Atatürk and his cadres to transform Turkey into a Westernized country, despite her socio-economic, political and cultural heritage. All reforms were passed under conditions of martial law by a pragmatic leader and government with autocratic power. Popular mobilization and feminist demands for these reforms were absent. Women were emancipated by the decision of men. The extent to which these changes were absorbed into the socio-cultural fabric of Turkey will be taken up in Chapter 3.

---

* The reader should note that, in the following historical account and subsequent sociological analysis, the specific subject matter is Turkish society in general, and Turkish women in particular – regardless of any possible similarities with Armenian, Assyrian and Kurdish people that may or may not exist. Nor, therefore, has it been judged necessary to recount either past or present day events affecting the Kurdish and Armenian communities living in Anatolia, now modern Turkey.

2. Islam and the Honour Ethic

Islam

Islam, as a belief system, corresponds to the socio-political conditions on the Arabian Peninsula in the seventh century AD. Islamic belief spread rapidly thereafter into many areas. In recent decades Islam has become common in Europe and is growing at a faster rate than any other religion in the world. Little is known in Europe of Islamic history and dogma. In fact, it is a continuation of the Judaeo-Christian tradition carried to its logical outcome. Islam simplified and structured the Judaeo-Christian message, broke any lingering bonds with paganism, chiselled away symbolic frills and structured monotheism into an absolute dogma.

Islam is the primary religion in Middle Eastern and North African countries, the northern parts of black Africa and in south, southeast and central Asia. It is the largest minority religion in India, China, the Philippines and the former Soviet Union. It has also become the second largest religion in North America and Western Europe. It is estimated that there are about 810 million people in predominantly Muslim countries. When Muslim populations living as minorities in other countries are added, the total estimated number is over one billion. As such, Islam is one of the three most prevalent religions in the world, after Christianity and Buddhism.

The estimated number of Muslims in Europe, including Eastern Europe, is 24 million. About two-thirds of this population consists of native Muslims in the Balkan Peninsula and the European part of the former Soviet Union. The great majority of Muslims in Western Europe are immigrant workers from Muslim countries. As many as six million Muslims are believed to have settled in Western Europe during the last three decades (Slomp, 1988). The estimated distribution of Muslims in some Western European countries is presented in Table 2.1 (Sander, 1988a). The majority of Muslims in Sweden, Denmark, Finland (Tartars), the Netherlands, Switzerland, Austria and Germany are Turks.

Turks accepted Islam at a relatively late stage and, since the early Middle Ages, have had the closest relations with Europe of any Muslim people, as evidenced in the expression 'the Muslim in Europe has always had a Turkish face' (Slomp, 1988). Islam has had a profound influence on Turkish culture and

Table 2.1. Estimated number of Muslims in some Western European countries

Country	Number of Muslims	As % of total population
Austria	70,000	0.9
Belgium	250,000	2.5
Denmark	40,000	0.8
Finland	1,500	
France	2,450,000	4.5
Great Britain	1,000,000	1.7
The Netherlands	300,000	2.1
Norway	15,000	0.36
Sweden	45,000	0.5
Switzerland	60,000	0.9
West Germany	1,900,000	3.0

Source: Sandera, 1988.

the status of women. This chapter summarizes the birth of Islam, and the ideological and practical changes it has brought to the lives of women.

The Arabian Peninsula AD 600

In the seventh century, when Islam was founded, the Arabian Peninsula was divided into two distinct areas. Several civilizations had developed in the southern part of the Peninsula where climatic conditions were favourable. The kingdoms of Sheba and Hadramut were known to have existed as early as the seventh century BC. These peoples were sedentary. They believed in a theological trio consisting of a moon god, a sun goddess and a god of the stars. Christianity and Judaism were also commonly practised in the southern Peninsula.

The peoples of the central and northern parts of the Peninsula were mostly Bedouins, living as nomadic tribes. A few sparsely populated settlements, such as the towns of Mecca and Medina, served as trade centres in what is now Saudi Arabia. Detailed information about Bedouin religious beliefs is not available. Poetry and the few written documents from the pre-Islamic period suggest that piety was not a dominant characteristic in their belief systems. Although there were a few tribes that had converted to Christianity and/or Judaism, most tribes were polytheistic. The most important pre-Islamic god was Allah who was believed to determine the climate, life, death and fate. The Arabic word 'Allah' means God. It was believed that Allah was assisted by three goddesses, Allat, Manat and Aluzza. Each tribe, and even each family, in addition had its own gods who were believed to protect them from hostile neighbours. The basic method of worship was to sacrifice cattle to the gods. Temples were few; instead there were shrines, where the gods were believed to reside, which could be visited for animal sacrifices.

There was one temple of great significance: the Kaaba in Mecca. This building originally consisted of a rectangular area surrounded by walls. It had no roof or windows. The Koran says that this was the first sacred building on earth (Koran 3:96). It is believed that Adam started construction of the building. After falling into disrepair, it was restored and completed by Abraham. Muslims, while praying, always turn their face in the direction of the Kaaba. Before the take-over of Mecca by Muslims, the Kaaba was used as a polytheistic temple that housed pictures and statues of the various deities. It also contained a meteorite which became Islam's hallowed Black Stone.

Muhammed and his *sunna*

The Islamic calendar begins with the year AD 622. This is the year Muhammed moved from Mecca to Medina. The events that lead to the prophecy of Muhammed started 12 years earlier. Muhammed, often called the Prophet (570?–632), was born in Mecca. He belonged to the Hashimite family of the Koreish tribe. His father died before his birth and he lost his mother when he was six. He was brought up by a paternal uncle. He grew up and lived as a poor man until, at the age of 25, he married a wealthy woman named Hadija. He, thereafter, engaged in his wife's trading enterprise and lived a financially comfortable life. It is believed that both Muhammed and his wife had monotheistic inclinations. Some of Hadija's close relatives were converts to Christianity, or *hanif* (monotheistic). Both were known not to worship any idol or make pagan sacrifices. They also were known to spend much time in meditation.

Muhammed and his family used to spend a month every summer on Mount Hira near Mecca. It was on this mountain, in the month of Ramadan AD 610, that Muhammed, at the age of 41, received his first revelation. Traditional accounts relate that Muhammed was taking a contemplative nap in a cave on the mountain when, in a dream, the angel Gabriel appeared to him, carrying a green banner with some script on it. Gabriel ordered him to read it but Muhammed had received no formal education and was illiterate. He answered that he was unable to read, but Gabriel repeated the order. Muhammed answered in the same way. These words were exchanged for a third time and, then, the first verses of the 96th Sura were revealed:

> Recite in the name of your Lord who created, created man from clots of blood!
> Recite! Your Lord is the Most Bountiful One, who by the pen taught man what he did not know. (Dawood, 1974)

Muhammed awoke and ran out of the cave. To his astonishment, he saw that the whole sky and the horizon were covered with the image of Gabriel carrying the green banner, still ordering him to read! After Muhammed repeatedly stated that he was illiterate, Gabriel finally read to him what was written on the banner:

Say: 'God is One, the Eternal One. He begot none, nor was He begotten. None is equal to Him'. (Koran 112; Dawood, 1974)

Gabriel told Muhammed that he was to be God's messenger. Nobody knows how long Muhammed stood there. When his return was delayed, Hadija sent people to search for him. They found him standing on a cliff, gazing at the sky. Upon returning to his wife, Muhammed told her of his dream and the subsequent vision. He was agitated. He believed that he had had an hallucination. It is said that Hadija was not surprised at Muhammed's experience, but rejoiced, interpreting the event as a prophecy. In order to be sure, they consulted one of Hadija's cousins, a learned *hanif*. He confirmed that it was probably no hallucination, because it was so similar to the message received by Moses. Hadija was the first to convert to 'Muhammed's religion'.

During the early years, it was not clear whether revelations to Muhammed were a continuation of Judaism or Christianity, or if they represented a new religion. The revelations to Muhammed had concerned only the singularity of God and, in content, very much resembled the Old Testament. In the beginning, Muhammed identified himself as hanif – neither a Jew nor a Christian. He sought collaboration with the Jewish and Christian tribes in the region in his fight against polytheism but did not receive much assistance.

The characteristics that distinguish Islam as a religion different from Judaism and Christianity emerged in later years, after Muhammed and his adherents moved to Medina. Islam gradually began identifying itself with the religion of Abraham, the first monotheist, who was 'neither Jew nor Christian'. God was defined by Abraham as one, merciful, beyond comprehension by the human mind and with a will no human could change, question or supplant. Abraham's example of total submission to the instructions of the only God was to be followed. The word 'Islam' means submission: a Muslim is a person who completely submits only to the authority of God.

Islam accepts the traditional belief that the founders of Judaism and Christianity (Abraham, Moses, David and Jesus) received from God: that they were the 'chosen' ones who communicated God's Word to their followers. On four occasions, the Word became a Book (thus the term 'people of the book', see section on umma). Koranic accounts about the prophets are the same as in the Jewish Torah and the Christian Bible. Islam differs in the manner in which Jews and Christians have interpreted the message and how they have applied the laws of God.

For instance, Muslims believe that Jesus was sent by God to deliver the good news and that he was born of a virgin:

'I am the messenger of your Lord,' he replied, 'and have come to give you a holy son.'

'How shall I bear the child,' she answered, 'when I am a virgin, untouched by man?'

'Such is the will of your Lord,' he replied. 'That is no difficult thing for Him. "He shall be a sign to mankind," says the Lord, "and a blessing from Ourself. This is our decree."'

Thereupon she conceived Him, and retired to a far-off place. (Koran 19:22; Dawood, 1974)

Islamic belief differs from the Christian interpretation of this event. Although he was cherished by God and created by God's will, Islamic theology holds that Jesus was not God's son ('He begot none, nor was he begotten'). Islam maintains that Christians misinterpreted the message as they do not believe in the singularity of God, but in the holy trinity. Koranic doctrine states that Jews also misinterpreted the message, particularly by not believing in, and following, Jesus (Koran 19:34). The final separation of Islam from other religions became clear in the 109th Sura:

'You have your own religion, and I have mine.' (Koran 109:6; Dawood, 1974)

During his ten years in Mecca following the first revelation, few people except for Muhammed's closest family members and friends converted to his interpretation of monotheism. Not only were Meccans, in general, resistant to his message, but there were also rumours of a conspiracy against Muhammed's life. His own tribe, the Koreish, opposed his message for fear of losing their control over the city. Muhammed preached equality, rejected any kind of human authority and demanded of people that they be loyal only to God. What Muhammed preached threatened the existing narrow tribal and family interests because it called on people to transcend worldly forms of submission and authority, and to unite in one belief, one order, one absolute truth.

As his difficulties in Mecca increased, Muhammed received an invitation from adherents in Medina, where the majority of the city's inhabitants had converted. In 622, Muhammed and his entourage escaped from Mecca to Medina, where Muhammed lived for the final ten years of his life. The migration is a turning point in Islamic history because it was after this that the religion assumed its complete doctrine and began to spread.

While the revelations during the years in Mecca had been mainly anti-polytheistic, those received in Medina shaped the character of Islam to confront the questions of practical life. Revelations concerning women were communicated in Medina. The first Islamic army was organized to protect the community from polytheist aggression. Concepts of holy war (*jihad*) and martyrdom (*shadat*) were formulated: God's will and justice, as revealed in the Koran, would be defended even if it involved struggle. Islam began taking its specific shape.

Islam was a powerful weapon against the tribal conflicts which disrupted unity and prevented the concentration of wealth and power on the Arabian Peninsula. Working together towards common goals was necessary for survival there because of its sparse resources. The nature of tribal morality was such that it perpetuated conflicts and hindered unity. This morality corresponded to polytheistic ideology: the multitude of gods were inconsistent, capricious entities who could sometimes be benevolent, sometimes cruel. The actions of the gods could not be predicted as they were not bound by principles that defined what was absolutely good or bad. People behaved like the gods they worshipped. Their tribal allegiance defined the limits of their morality. There existed no framework of principles, no absolute good or bad. The fact that what was good for one tribe or family may have had devastating effects on another was of no concern to polytheists.

The existence of a large number of tribes, each seeking narrow ends and struggling with others to reach those ends, was hindering the establishment of a larger community of common interest for increased prosperity, better exploitation of limited resources and accumulation of wealth. The narrow, selfish tribal morality inspired by belief in the unpredictable, capricious behaviour of the gods needed to be replaced by a universal and unalterable morality prescribed by an absolute wisdom, which was consistent. In order to put an end to the blood feuds between tribes, for instance, murder had to be pronounced evil under all circumstances, not just if it occurred within the tribe. Only such an altruistic morality could put an end to conflicts and unite the people.

Islamic ideology preached that tribal allegiance should be directed to an umma, or an ideological group based on common belief. Islam sought 'to transfer a group of individuals into a community of believers' (Mernissi, 1985) in an economic and political system administered by one single will, one single morality, one single decision-maker: God. Islam promised an entirely new order on the Arabian peninsula.

Muhammed was a man of great organizational abilities, as well as being a great political leader. His leadership extended into all areas of life. Through his *sunna* (example) he established norms for everything, from the simplest tasks for the management of daily life to the complexities of legal and state matters. Much of his sunna and the Koran verses, which later became customary or compulsory for Muslims in regard to daily activities, were just common sense. Examples are: keeping one's body clean (compulsory washing of the face, neck and extremities five times daily, before each prayer; bathing after intercourse); prohibiting eating pork (which was the primary source of trichinosis, a debilitating disease); brushing teeth; prohibiting alcohol, and so on. It is recorded that he would run, with his wife Aisha, every afternoon in order to show his umma the importance of keeping one's body fit (Demircan, 1985). Reading the *Hadis*, the volumes where Muhammed's sunna are recorded, is informative: one learns the extent to which this remarkable person went to demonstrate an example of spiritual and physical well-being as he struggled to establish a new society.

After two years in Medina, Muhammed's position was considerably strengthened. Significant numbers of Jewish and Christian tribes had accepted Islamic beliefs and polytheism had been greatly reduced. Muhammed began planning for a take-over of Mecca, which was still under polytheistic control. An agreement was negotiated in 628 which allowed Muslims to visit the city. Their work to promote Islam allowed a peaceful assumption of control two years later. Muhammed entered the Kaaba, the temple of Adam and Abraham, cleansed it of all idols and pictures, and led the first Muslim congregation in prayer.

The religious–political take-over of Mecca signified a notable victory for Islam. Within a short time, the entire Arabian Peninsula was under Muslim control. Polytheism was eradicated. Other monotheist 'nations' (umma) were allowed sovereign existence under Muslim protection. In 632, two years after the take-over of Mecca, Muhammed made his second and last pilgrimage (*haj*) to the city. He died the same year, at the age of 64. He left behind the 'Word', which later was organized and written as the Koran, and a united Islamic state, which later became an empire.

The struggle over the caliphate

Muhammed had no living sons at the time of his death. His closest paternal relative was his cousin, Ali, who was married to Muhammed's daughter, Fatima. At that time, Ali was a young man, so Muhammed's uncle and father-in-law, Abu Bakr, as a respected older person, was chosen to take over Muhammed's duties as religious leader (*caliph*). He died two years later and was succeeded by Omar. It was during the ten years under Omar's caliphate (634–644) that important Islamic institutions were organized, including Islamic higher education, a taxation system and welfare organizations. The first Islamic law (*Sheria*) was written and schools of law were established. Also during this time, Islamic expansion reached north in the Middle East and west into North Africa.

Omar was assassinated and his reign was followed by that of Osman. During 12 years of Osman's caliphate, further institutionalization occurred. The 114 Suras revealed to Muhammed by Gabriel were compiled into the Koran (which means book, reading), and the *Hadis* (communication, narrative) were written. Six collections of *Hadis* constitute the *Sunna*, the practice and sayings of Muhammed which provide guidance for adherents.

Following the death of Osman in 656, those who were dissatisfied with the succession of caliphs wanted Ali to assume control. By this time, Ali was a mature man. Not only had he been one of the first converts to Islam, and a person who had been very close to Muhammed while he lived, but he was also the father of Muhammed's grandchildren. Supported by his followers, who had organized as *Shiat-ul Ali* (Ali's party), Ali formally put up his candidacy for the caliphate. Several other people, notably Muhammed's widow Aisha, were opposed to him holding the office. An old feud between herself and Ali (the *Ifk* incident, see p. 47) is said to have gone so far as to lead her to take up arms in an unsuccessful uprising against Ali in what became known as the Camel Battle. Ali was assassinated in Kuf'a and Muawiye, the governor of Syria, declared himself Caliph.

The assassination of Ali led to the first Islamic schism between the Sunni and Shiite groups. The Shiites had supported Ali's candidacy and did not accept the caliphate of Muawiye. In 680, Ali's son (Muhammed's grandson), Husayn, revolted against the Sunni caliphate. He and his soldiers were ambushed by the new Sunni Caliph Yazid on the Kerbela desert and brutally killed when he refused to surrender.

The murder of Muhammed's grandson, and the deceit surrounding it, is one of the most grievous events in Islamic history, mourned by both the Sunnis and the Shiites. The Shiites have never forgiven the Sunnis for having caused the death of Husayn. Shiites commemorate the martyrdom of Ali and Husayn every year. Ali is considered a great warrior and a mystic who was the only person, apart from Muhammed, with an esoteric interpretation of the Koran. Shiites have a cult of martyrdom, suffering and revolt, which is not shared by the Sunnis. The Shiite sect is considered the more radical of the two. Shiite thinking has strongly inspired Islamic mysticism and heterodox interpretations of the religion. Ideas such as martyrdom, suffering in the service of God, the right to revolt and so on, have provided fertile soil for mystical sects such as the Sufi, Alevi and Bektashi orders of Anatolia which are explained below. The attitude of Sunnis and Shiites to the status of women, however, is the same.

After the schism
In spite of inner strife, Islam continued to spread and empires arose. In the west, leadership of Islamic Sunni empires was represented first by Arabs and then by Turks. In the east, leadership was represented by the Persian Shiites. During more than 1000 years, stable Islamic civilizations with their own legal, economic and educational systems arose. Arts and sciences flourished. From the 1600s, these systems began to erode as a result of the growing success of European states. Under their influence, often accompanied by threats and military aggression, Islamic traditions began to be modified, mostly in the economic sphere. Family structure and the status of men and women have been most resistant to change, probably because the organization of these spheres of life is of central importance to patriarchies. The world has always been under the control of men, whether Eastern or Western, who have perceived women as an extension of themselves.

In Muslim countries today, ideologies ranging from orthodox funda-mentalism to radical Marxism exist. Whatever the individual or group tendencies may be, it is impossible to ignore the impact of Islamic dogma on society and its political and practical implications (Hjärpe, 1984).

The basics of Islam

> The Exordium. In the name of God the compassionate and merciful. Praise be to God, Lord of the creation, the compassionate, the merciful, King of Judgement-day! You alone we worship, and to You alone we pray for help. Guide us to the straight path, the path of those whom You have favoured, not of those who have incurred Your wrath, nor of those who have gone astray. (Koran 1; Dawood, 1974)

These are the opening verses of the Koran. There are five dogmatic principles in Islamic belief. They are as follows: (1) the oneness and omnipotence of God; (2) the acceptance of Muhammed as the messenger of God; (3) the Koran is the revealed word of God; (4) there is a hierarchy of angels headed by Gabriel who dictated the Koran to Muhammed; and (5) there will be a judgement day and human souls are immortal.

There are five religious duties (pillars) of Islam: (1) acceptance of the unity of God and that Muhammed is his messenger; (2) to pray five times each day, at predetermined times; (3) to donate the equivalent of 2.5% of one's annual income as charity (*zakat*); (4) to fast from sunrise to sunset during one month every year (*Ramadan*); and (5) to visit the Kaaba once in a lifetime (*haj*). The requirement to witness the unity of God and the message of Muhammed is essential for every Muslim. The other requirements are conditional: prayers and fasting are required for healthy adults; alms-giving is required of those who have an income; and the pilgrimage to Mecca is required only if it does not place inordinate hardship on the traveller or his or her family.

Islam is strongly monotheistic: 'No God but God' is the most often repeated formula. As such, it not only refutes pagan polytheism but also Christianity (with its Father-Son-Holy Ghost triumvirate) and mystical interpretations of Islam. God has immaculate qualities which have been revealed in the Koran. These qualities cannot be possessed, shared or imitated. It is God who creates, gives life and takes it away, and knows the absolute truth. The truth has been revealed by God through the prophets and the sacred books. Earlier monotheistic communities (not their prophets) have misinterpreted God's message (Koran 19:34). That is why God communicated the fourth book, the Koran, which contains the absolute truth. Muslims believe that the Koran was communicated directly from God and Muhammed's role was only that of a messenger. It is God who speaks through the texts. Muslims must, to avoid the 'mistakes' made by earlier monotheists, submit themselves totally to the words of the Koran. Hence, the word Islam, which means 'submission', evolved as the proper noun describing the religion. Islamic law is based on the Koran.

At the risk of over-simplification, it can be said that the above characteristic lies at the heart of Islam's so-called 'political' nature. In practice, this means that the precepts communicated in the Koran, and the Islamic social order based on them, may not be questioned or modified. The content of the Koran cannot be reinterpreted. The religion cannot be reformed. Islam rejects all rules and systems constructed by humans – not based on the rules of the Koran – as unnatural and leading to the enslavement of humans by humans. Because human systems may not be based on an absolute truth, there is risk of submission to a false truth, or to evil. From a fundamentalist Muslim's perspective, expecting humans to follow unnatural man-made rules, instead of obeying only God's order, is tyranny (*zulm*). Thus, all man-made political and social systems are considered tyrannical. These include all secular systems, under which Muslims are given the right – indeed have the duty – to revolt in a holy war, in order to re-establish the rule of God.

There is considerable scepticism in Islam about human initiative. To question or attempt to change the Islamic order may be interpreted as a revolt against God. This is probably why Islam has not undergone any reformation. It should be added that scepticism about individual initiative is not based on a belief that human beings are prone to immorality and evil: it is based on the belief that living in the most perfect system should be sufficient and people should not have to search for new alternatives.

This short and simplified account of the basic principles of Islamic thought is defended by fundamentalists. There are, of course, other religious groups within Islam which argue that reform is possible. The fundamentalists and reformists often engage in discussions, quoting the Koran against the Koran, the sunna against the sunna, to prove their points. Each group can find support for their stand by an eclectic selection of the guiding verses (Hjärpe, 1983; Nordberg, 1988). Groups that would like to introduce quick, radical change find working for reform in Islam to be extremely difficult. That is why these groups take a secularist stand, proposing, as did the Kemalist republicans of Turkey, the total elimination of Islam from the legal arena. Whatever the differences, however, people living in countries with an Islamic history bear the remnants of the tradition. Nowhere is this more obvious than in the area of gender roles.

Heterodox Interpretations of Islam

The Anatolian Alevi and Bektashi movements

The Alevis and the Bektashi orders constitute an Anatolian version of the Shiite branch. Sunni Muslims consider these belief systems to be heretical. It is important to mention these movements because they have made important contributions to Anatolian Turkish folklore and also because of their very different attitudes towards women.

The Alevi sect was founded by Hadji Bektash Veli (1210–1260) in central Anatolia. Hadji Bektash is believed to have been a disciple of Baba Ishak, a Turkomen who, supported by the peasantry, led a revolt in 1240 against the sedentary Seljuk aristocracy. During this, as well as in other uprisings, the revolutionary element in Shiite dogma was used as an ideological motive to counteract the Sunni Seljuks. Hadji Bektash formulated an ideology which combined the characteristic features of Central Asian Turkomen beliefs together with some remnants of shamanism, and the revolutionary and martyrdom principles in Shiite dogma. Some Christian elements, taken from the formerly Christian Anatolian peasantry, also were incorporated (Brill, 1960).

Alevism is characterized primarily as the religion of the nomadic Turkomens who resisted the Ottoman central theocracy. It spread in the Anatolian and Balkan countryside among the peasantry as a result of the Seljuk and Ottoman policies of forced settlement. In the beginning of the 1500s, Balim Sultan, originally a Greek Orthodox Christian, introduced Alevi thought in the artisan lodges and the Janissary Corps. These latter groups, who adopted Alevi thought, are called the Bektashis (Alevism is an in-group religion acquired by birth: converts to it become Bektashi). The Bektashi movement contributed to the spread of Alevi thought among urban populations and on the Balkan Peninsula (Gökalp, 1980).

The fact that both the Alevis in the countryside and the Bektashis in the cities used a pure Turkish language in their prose – as opposed to the language of the Ottoman aristocracy which was a mixture of Arabic and Persian, unintelligible to the common people – has contributed to these movements gaining wide acceptance. Alevi-Bektashi beliefs include elements of Islamic mysticism (Sufism), which more liberally interprets the principles of Islam. Contrary to aristocratic Sufi traditions, however, Alevi thought is identified with the Turkish–Anatolian peasantry, the formerly Christian janissaries and urban artisans.

The Alevi sect and the Bektashi order are significant because of their attitude towards women. They do not practise gender segregation or polygyny. Women are not veiled. Women and men participate together in religious ceremonies and meetings where matters concerning individual behaviour or the community are discussed collectively. During ceremonies, men and women drink wine, dance and sing together. Because they do not enforce strict gender segregation, which is one of the corner-stones of Islamic practice, the Alevis and Bektashis are unique. They are, in fact, considered heretics especially by the Sunni majority. Throughout the centuries, the Sunnis have been strongly prejudiced against these groups, accusing them of immorality because of the absence of gender segregation and because women have enjoyed a greater degree of autonomy (Gökalp, 1980; Brill, 1960).

The absence of gender segregation is probably a survival of shamanic traditions. There are a large number of shaman characteristics in the Alevi tradition such as: rituals that simulate rebirth after death; reincarnation of the soul in an animal or plant; beliefs about the sacredness of certain animals (particularly hares, deer and bear), some mountains and the hearth. It also has elements reminiscent of Christianity, such as the belief in a holy trinity consisting of God, Muhammed and Ali; distribution of wine, bread and cheese at religious ceremonies; confession and absolution offered by religious leaders (the *dede*), and some practice of celibacy (Hassan, 1985; Gökalp, 1980; Brill, 1960).

The Ottomans considered Alevism as heresy, to be eradicated from Anatolia. Sultan Selim I challenged the Alevis from 1517 to 1520, when he massacred about 40,000 Alevis in Anatolia, followed by an attack on Shiite Persia, the subjugation of Egypt and the assumption of the title of caliph. The Bektashi order received a great blow when Sultan Mahmut II, in an attempt to reform the army, abolished the Janissary Corps in a bloody massacre in 1826.

It is estimated there are about 10–12 million Alevis in Turkey at present, mostly living in areas between the Kizilirmak and the Euphrates Rivers and in the Aegean and Mediterranean regions of the country. Alevi and Bektashi thought has had a profound effect on Anatolian beliefs and folklore. Even those who reject their dogma share a variety of Alevi beliefs and practices, recite their powerful poetry and sing their songs in clear, lyrical Turkish. Alevism is strictly a Turkish–Anatolian phenomenon which spread further into the Balkan Peninsula, particularly Albania, through the Bektashi order.

The acceptance that these interpretations of Islam gained from large portions of society can perhaps partially explain how Turkey, at the beginning of the twentieth century, was able to introduce very radical reforms in a theocratic Sunni society, thereby becoming the first Muslim country to choose secularization and to give women equal legal rights (Gökalp, 1980). The following piece of poetry reflects the pursuit of gender equality in Alevi–Bektashi thought:

Hey men, we are as good as any of you
Because we know how to show respect that is true
Along the same path we are united with you
Do not exaggerate this barren issue

True, in clothing we are separates
But in fact we are not your servants
Let it be known, we shall regard as fools
Those of you who think we are inferiors.

(Gölpinarli, 1963)

Sufism

Muhammed was neither an ascetic nor a mystic. He preached modesty and moderation rather than asceticism. The image of God he portrayed was objective: he never identified himself as being a reflection or part of God. He always carefully avoided making far-fetched interpretations of Islamic teachings or the nature of creation. Nevertheless, an Islamic mysticism came into being. The first ascetics appeared a few centuries after the birth of Islam, probably in response to the luxurious life of the caliphs. The need to add new dimensions to the orthodox, narrow-minded Sunni interpretation of the Koran may also have motivated them.

The central point of Sufi thought is love of God. Adherents do not serve God for fear of hell or out of a feeling of obligation: God is loved by the Sufis because they see God in everything. They believe that they come from, and one day shall be united with, God. Sufis describe life on earth in platonic terms, as a period of passage and suffering before, once again, being united with God. They have little reverence for secular rules, rather they try to establish a perfect relationship with God. Asceticism, meditation, fasting as well as poetry, dancing and wine are part of Sufi rituals.

Among the more famous Sufis are Gazali (1058–1111) who wrote several very important philosophical books; Omar Khayyam (died circa 1123), whose profane poetry was much appreciated; Ibn Arabi (1165–1240), who wrote important treatises and poetry exploring the relationship between the senses and creation; Mevlana (1207–1273), a Persian who lived in Anatolia, who produced one of the most important books of Islamic literature (the *Mesnevi*) and established the order of 'the whirling dervishes'; Rabia of Basra (died 801), the only Muslim woman who reached the status of sainthood in spite of the fact that she was not a mother or wife and dedicated herself to spinsterhood and worship; and Halladji Mansur (died 922), who was lynched because he suggested that he was God (Ringgren and Åström, 1978).

Sufis were kind to women. In some mystical essays, there are views to the effect that women are more important than men. The belief that God might have female attributes is evidenced in some of their writings:

> Hence to contemplate the Absolute in woman is to see both aspects simultaneously, and such a vision is more perfect than seeing [God] in all the forms in which it manifests itself. That is why woman is creative, not created. . . . Both qualities, active and passive, belong to the Creator, and both are manifested in woman. (From the *Mesnevi*, Bakhtiyar, 1987)

Perhaps this more lenient approach was one reason why Islamic mysticism attracted many learned Anatolian women. Even though the Sufi orders were dominated by men, women were tolerated, which gave them an opportunity for intellectual development within the orders (Schimmel, 1982).

Women and Islam

There is a tendency in Western societies to regard Islam as the epitome of misogyny, which is true in so far as monotheism, in particular, and patriarchy, in general, are misogynous. It is actually impossible to judge, with any objectivity, whether the misogyny in Islam is greater or less than that in other patriarchal systems. It is generally accepted that, in some areas concerning women and sexuality (as well as other spheres of life), the Islamic approach has been more progressive than the Judaeo-Christian tradition. This was particularly true of Christianity as it was practised in the Middle Ages and at the beginning of the Reformation. Muslim theologians, for instance, did not discuss whether women were human or whether they had souls; the mass slaughter of women for the contrived crime of practising witchcraft has not occurred in the Islamic world (Armstrong, 1987).

When a fundamentalist today preaches that women ought to behave as prescribed in the seventh century, Islamic thought about women can hardly be said to be progressive. It must be remembered, however, that viewed in the context of the socio-political conditions prevailing in Europe and the Middle East 1400 years ago, Islam was a force which improved the lot of women.

Muslims have two main sources of religious inspiration: the Koran is primary; secondary are the 'examples' Muhammed demonstrated to his adherents through his behaviour and interpretation of the revelations. These are based on the witness of people who knew Muhammed and collected in the *Hadis*. They contain rich information on Muhammed's thoughts about, and treatment of, women.

Muhammed and women

> Three things in life are dear to me: perfume, women and prayer –
> Muhammed.

Muhammed was an erotic man, highly vulnerable and susceptible to women. He took nine wives (or twelve, according to some authors) during his lifetime. He was the only Muslim allowed to marry more than four women (Koran 33:50). It was subsequently revealed to him that he should neither marry any more women nor divorce any of his existing wives (Koran 33:52). The number of concubines he had is unknown, but they may have been few, because Muhammed was opposed to slavery and tried to set an example by marrying his female slaves and freeing the males (Koran 24:33).

Of all his wives, he was most fond of Hadija, his first wife, and Aisha, the last. Hadija was a wealthy and intelligent woman. She was a widow. Muhammed was her employee, supervising her trade caravans to Damascus, when she took the initiative and proposed marriage to him. Hadija was 40 years old and Muhammed was 25 when they got married. She was the first person to convert to Islam. She also gave birth to all his children except one. They stayed married for 25 years, until Hadija's death. During his marriage to Hadija, Muhammed did not take any other wife.

He thereafter took eight wives (or eleven by other accounts) during the course of about a decade. Most of these marriages were politically inspired or to set an example as the protector of women (Hjärpe, 1984). Some, such as that to Zeinep, were based on attraction. Zeinep was the wife of Zeid, an ex-slave whom Muhammed had adopted as a son. One day Muhammed saw Zeinep unveiled and was shaken by her beauty. Zeid noticed that his adoptive father was attracted to his wife. Out of gratitude to Muhammed, Zeid offered to divorce Zeinep so Muhammed could marry her. Because of an earlier Koranic revelation, which prohibited men from marrying their former daughters-in-law, Muhammed could not accept Zeid's offer. At this time a new revelation came to Muhammed, stating there were no restrictions against men marrying the ex-wives of adopted sons, and that God wished Muhammed to marry Zeinep in order to set an example (Koran 33:37). Upon hearing of this Zeid divorced his wife and she married Muhammed.

Muhammed's most beloved wife, Aisha, was the daughter of the powerful and prestigious Abu Bakr, who after Muhammed's death became the first caliph. She was the only virgin Muhammed married (all his other wives had either been widows or divorcees). It is believed that at the time of marriage, Aisha was 6 and Muhammed 54 years old (the marriage was not consummated until three years later, when Aisha reached puberty). Muhammed loved her dearly and made it no secret that he favoured her. She was an intelligent, quick-witted woman, who exercised considerable political and religious power during and after Muhammed's lifetime.

Verses relating to Muhammed's wives appear primarily in the 33rd Sura of the Koran. This sura, in light of the Hadis and Muhammed's biography, reveals a man who often had mundane problems in his polygamous family, just as any other husband in the same situation might have. Some verses aim at restoring harmony in his family. For instance, one verse (33:28) scolds his wives for putting too much pressure on him to buy them jewellery and other adornments. In another, two of his wives (Aisha and Hafsa) are reproached for conspiring and gossiping (Koran 66:3–5), an incident that distressed Muhammed so much that he left all his wives for a month.

Verse 4:3 of the Koran, which permits polygyny, also obliges men to treat all their wives with absolute emotional and material equality. Husbands are warned against favouritism and advised to refrain from taking new wives if they feel they cannot avoid having favourites. In practice, this means a husband must spend an equal number of nights with, and pay an equal amount of attention to, every wife. Adhering to this verse was very difficult for Muhammed: he did have one favourite wife (Aisha) with whom he wanted to spend more time than with the others. In one revelation (Koran 33:51), he was allowed to delay visiting his less appreciated wives. After that revelation, he spent almost all his time with Aisha, particularly his last days. He died in her house and was buried there. He was also exempted from paying *mehir*, the marriage payment, to one woman who had proposed marriage to him. It is said that such situations led Aisha to revolt with the words: 'God seems to grant revelations according to your lusts' (Hadis no. 1721, Buhari, tefsir 7).

In the Hadis, it is often mentioned that Muhammed was a very tolerant husband. His wives frequently argued with and disobeyed him. Aisha was a particularly strong personality who would challenge his judgements, even the Koranic revelations. When others criticized, he defended Aisha's special privilege by admonishing: 'Do not sadden me because of Aisha. It is only in her room that I get revelations'. During a visit, Aisha's father, Abu Bakr, was so upset with Aisha's treatment of the Prophet, that he slapped her for talking back to her husband. Upon observing this, Muhammed reproached Abu Bakr, saying it was not up to him to decide how Aisha should treat her husband.

Muhammed took a wife everywhere he went. War was no exception. On one such excursion, Aisha happened to wander away from the caravan at night and got lost in the desert. She was later found by a young man, who took her on his camel and brought her back to Muhammed. After this, a rumour began to spread that Aisha, who had spent a whole night alone with the young man in the desert, might have committed adultery. Aisha denied it, but the rumour was persistent. Ali, Muhammed's son-in-law, insisted that Muhammed divorce Aisha. This was the beginning of the hostilities between Ali and Aisha which were to play an important role in the Shiite–Sunni schism later on. Muhammed was greatly distressed, for he believed in Aisha and did not want to be separated from her. About this time, there came the revelation demanding that the charge of adultery be proved by no less than four male eye-witnesses who had actually seen the couple having intercourse, or that those who slander be severely punished. Eight verses followed, strongly condemning those who spread rumours about Aisha (Koran 24:11–19). The rumours ended abruptly and the marriage was saved.

Muhammed was not immune to earthly problems, neither did he attempt to hide his vulnerability. He even opposed the Koran when he felt his family pride threatened. Having married so many women himself, he was very angered to hear that his son-in-law, Ali, was planning to take a second wife in addition to Muhammed's daughter, Fatma. He burst out to a congregation, that he would, under no circumstances, tolerate that even if it was written in the Book. He is quoted as having said:

> May God forgive me! But even God cannot expect me to let my daughter have a rival! Fatma can get a divorce and return to my protection whenever she wishes! (Demircan, 1985)

Ali's plans to marry a second woman were effectively stopped after that outburst from his powerful father-in-law.

Muhammed's personality resembled that of a kindly dictator or a liberal patriarch. When arranging gender relationships, patriarchal interests were definitely given priority. In verse 4:34, the husband is allowed to beat his wife. Muhammed later qualifies how a woman should be beaten. It should be done so that no bleeding or any other visible injury is inflicted, and a woman should be punished in this way only if she refuses sex. During his lifetime, Muhammed was lenient towards women, refraining from taking measures harsher than those suggested in the Koran, and trying to set an example for other men to be as tolerant towards women as possible within the patriarchal Islamic framework. Muhammed was aware that the evolving Islamic social order would not eliminate hardship for women, so he cautioned men against abuse of authority in one of the last sentences he uttered before his death: 'Be careful not to neglect three things: the daily prayer, the rights of slaves and the rights of women. . . . Because they are prisoners in your hands' (Imam Gazali, one of the foremost interpreters of the Sunna, see Müftüoglu, 1981).

After Muhammed's death, there was a general hardening of attitudes against women. During the time of the second caliph, Omar, the tone against women became significantly harsher. It appears that Omar was a misogynist. He is quoted as having said, 'Oppose women. Do not fulfil any of their wishes'; 'Do not provide clothes for women. Let them wear rags, so they will be too ashamed to go out of their tents'; and 'Let your wives get accustomed to the word "no"' (Gazali, see Müftüoglu, 1981). Aisha apparently collaborated in encouraging more restrictions on women. 'If,' she is quoted as having said, 'the Prophet had foreseen how women would begin behaving after his death, he would not have been as tolerant as he had been during his lifetime' (Gazali, see Müftüoglu, 1981).

Changes to the status of women
People who suggest that Islam initially brought improvements to the status of women on the Arabian Peninsula in the seventh century can find much support. Al-Tibri (1982) summarizes the changes Islam brought as follows:
• Female infanticide, which was widespread on the Peninsula before Islam,

was vehemently criticized and prohibited (Koran 16:58–60; 81:8,9); the killing of women which was not considered a serious crime before, was pronounced equally punishable (Koran 4:29). Women thus gained the right to live.
• Women were given the right to inherit a predetermined share of a descendant's property. Women and children had not previously had the right of inheritance. In some tribes, they were actually considered to be property that, at the death of their master, could be inherited by other men. Women gained the right to inherit half as much property as men (Koran 4:7–12,33).
• A woman's right to own property was ensured. It was prohibited to confiscate the property of widowed women and of orphan girls, as had sometimes been practised before Islam. All women gained the right to receive a payment (*mehir*) from their husbands at the time of marriage. If a wife was repudiated, her husband was obligated to compensate her with a second sum, very similar to alimony. Women gained the right to dispose of their property as they wished (Koran 4:4, 2:241) and were freed from earning a living for their families, which became the exclusive responsibility of men.
• Marriage rules were modified. Men were limited to four wives. This was not a material improvement because men still had the right to have extra-marital relationships with their female slaves. As noted above, men were warned against favouring any one wife over the others. They had to treat all of them equally in every respect (Koran 4:3). This was deemed an impossible task in another verse (Koran 4:129). These two verses are usually interpreted as actually limiting polygyny.
   Polygyny was not the only form of marriage before Islam. Polyandry also existed, under which a woman could marry up to ten men. If she became pregnant, she had the right to designate any one of her husbands as the child's father (El-Saadawi, 1980). That husband could not deny paternity. Women also had the right to initiate relationships with outstanding men in society in order to have children with them. These types of relationships were prohibited as prostitution in Islamic belief. The only forms of coexistence sanctioned by the Koran are monogamy and polygyny.
• Sexual rights were outlined. A woman was given the right to expect sexual gratification, and could get a divorce if she could prove that her husband had not had sexual relations with her for four months or that he was impotent. (In Turkey, women had a charming way of indicating in court that their husbands neglected them sexually: they removed a shoe and turned it upside down. This was usually enough for the court to grant a divorce to them immediately.) Men were prohibited from marrying the ex-wives of their fathers, neither could they marry two sisters at the same time. The period of waiting before remarriage for women (*iddet*) in the case of divorce, death or desertion of a husband, which formerly had been one year, was reduced to four months (to make sure that she was not pregnant by her ex-husband).
• Sexual norms of behaviour were set. These were organized in three groups. The first group (*farz*), was required of all Muslims and included marriage, regularity in sexual relations, covering of the body and parenthood. The second group consisted of prohibitions (*haram*): prostitution, adultery, premarital

relations, sodomy, homosexuality and celibacy. All types of behaviour and attitudes which might lead to these acts were also prohibited. The third group included practices which, although allowed in extreme cases, were not recommended: birth control, abortion, masturbation and divorce (Demircan, 1985).

The logic behind these rules is evident. Marriage is an important religious responsibility because it ensures regular sexual relations which will distract people from prohibited acts such as adultery or homosexuality, and because it will provide progeny. By the same token, celibacy is prohibited because it is in opposition to the requirement of marriage.

• New prohibitions were also passed such as against taking Muslim women as prisoners of war, expelling menstruating women from their homes and refusing to eat at the same table with them, and organizing and profiting from prostitution.

There is some indication that Muhammed tried to limit the 'Pharaoh infibulation', which involved the removal of the clitoris and labia minora of women as traditionally practised, particularly in Egypt and the Sudan. It is recorded that he warned a woman performing this operation against making 'cuts too deep' that 'would prevent a girl from feeling pleasure when she grows up' (Demircan, 1985). Clitoridectomy is not prescribed in the Koran, and, except for the above citation, there is no mention or approval of this practice in the Hadis. That Islam prescribes clitoridectomy is a misunderstanding. It certainly is not practised in the majority of Muslim societies. On the other hand, male circumcision is a traditional (not Koranic) requirement arising from the fact that the Prophet himself was circumcised as part of the semitic tradition. Male circumcision is prescribed by tradition because it is believed to increase pleasure and decrease the risk of venereal disease.

The image of women in Islam

It is not possible to discuss in depth in one chapter all aspects of Islamic thought and all rules concerning women and sexuality. As in other areas, Islam generally follows the Judaeo-Christian tradition. All three religions profess that man is superior to woman. Compare, for instance, the similarity between the following passages:

> Christ is supreme over every man, the husband is supreme over his wife (I Corinthians 11:3)

and:

> Women shall with justice have rights similar to those exercised against them, although men have a status above women. (Koran 2:228; Dawood, 1974)

Men are the masters of women in all three monotheistic religions. Even though, in the eyes of God, they are equal, on earth women are subordinate to men. This duality appears throughout the scriptures. Islam quantifies the inequality between men and women: in a court of law, the testimony of two women is equal to that of one man. In marriage, she is equal to one-fourth of a man.

There are subtle differences in the reasons for woman's subjugation and strategies for her salvation, which are necessary to understand the nature of the control mechanisms around Muslim women.

Eve

The myth of the 'original sin' being the fault of a woman, Eve, is a central concept in Judaeo-Christianity for explaining why women are inferior and deserve to suffer. It was Eve who caused the expulsion from Eden, and subjected humans to pain, sorrow, sickness and death. Because of this, woman is to suffer more than man and be dependent on him: 'In pains and anxieties dost thou bear children, woman; and toward thine husband is thy inclination and he lords over thee' (Genesis 3:16). It was because of the need to redeem the original sin, caused by woman, that God sent Jesus Christ who, through his suffering, atoned the original sin and won for man the possibility to reunite with God (Armstrong, 1987). By extension, woman is also responsible for the suffering of Jesus.

This myth is presented differently in the Koran. Eve is not mentioned by name, but only as 'Adam's wife'. Both are portrayed as victims of Satan. They are both cautioned not to eat from the tree (Koran 2:35, 7:19). Satan tempts both of them (Koran 20:121) and both of them, together with Satan, are expelled (Koran 20:121–2). In no instance is Adam's wife considered responsible for his temptation and neither are they doomed to suffer. When Adam repents he is forgiven, but remains on earth to fulfil the design of God's creation (Smith and Haddad, 1982). This difference may seem minor, but it is such very subtle differences between Judaeo-Christian tradition and Islam that eventually led to somewhat different conceptions of women and sexuality.

Freedom from guilt

That neither Adam nor Eve are doomed to eternal suffering, but are forgiven, is consistent with Islam's general view that life is not for suffering by either man or woman; that salvation on earth is possible; and that temptation and sex, when controlled by the social order, are essentially positive attributes. Mernissi (1985) explains this mechanism as follows:

> The Christian concept of the individual as tragically torn between two poles – good and evil, flesh and spirit, instinct and reason – is very different from the Muslim concept. Islam has a more sophisticated theory of the instincts, more akin to the Freudian concept of the libido. It views the raw instincts as energy. The energy of instincts is pure in the sense that it has no connotation to good or bad. The question of good or bad arises only when the social destiny of men is considered. The individual cannot survive except within a social order. Any social order has its set of laws. The set of laws decides which uses of the instincts are good or bad. It is the uses made of the

instincts, not the instincts themselves, that are beneficial or harmful to the social order. Therefore, in the Muslim order it is not necessary for the individual to eradicate his instincts or to control them for the sake of control itself, but he must use them according to the demands of the religious law.

Islam is a pragmatic religion. Contrary to Christian tradition, Islam is not concerned with the paradox of evil and suffering in a world created by an immaculate God. It maintains that evil would not exist so long as the natural needs of humans, as determined by God, are satisfied within the legal limits of his laws which organize the Muslim society. Thus, natural urges need not be suppressed or regulated by individuals. The individual does not have to feel guilty for having needs, or worry about how best to satisfy them. The social order, prescribed by God, provides the resolution.

Sex as worship

Islam considers sexuality to be a positive attribute: 'By another sign He gave you wives from among yourselves, that you might live in joy with them, and planted love and kindness in your hearts' (Koran 30:21; Dawood, 1974). In Islam, unsatisfied sexuality is a potential source of evil. This is indicated in the Hadis, where instructions about lovemaking are also given, based on the Prophet's sunna. This is also very different to the Christian attitude, where the sexual instinct was frequently described as evil. Armstrong (1987) explains how the Christian clergy linked sexuality with sin and advised celibacy as the best way to achieve salvation. St Paul, in his first letter to the Corinthians, states: 'A man does well not to marry' [and in anticipation of the imminent end of the world:] 'from now on married men should live as though they were not married' (I Corinthians 7:1,29).

Armstrong (1987) explains that it was believed that the avoidance of sex would enable an individual to direct more energy to the worship of God: 'An unmarried man concerns himself with the Lord's work, because he is trying to please the Lord; but a married man concerns himself with worldly matters, because he wants to please his wife' (I Corinthians 7:32-3). The belief that sexuality is sinful, led the Roman Catholic Church to pass an obligatory ruling for clerical celibacy in 1215. St Thomas Aquinas, who had a profound effect on Catholic thought, held that sex was always evil. Celibacy for both men and women was a sure way to salvation. For women, lifelong virginity was the most desirable state so that they might devote themselves totally to God. According to Armstrong (1987), Martin Luther also despised sex, even though he abolished celibacy in his reformed church. He stated that marriage only provides some remedy for man's uncontrollable lust.

Islam shuns celibacy, unless there is a physiological reason for it. Muhammed was a highly erotic man, who did not consider lust an evil burden. Such tendencies appear later in Islam. Imam Gazali (1058–1111), one of the foremost interpreters of the sunna, for instance, did consider lust a burden. He points out in his writings, however, that lust has a number of positive attributes, the most important being progeny. It also serves the divine purpose of giving men a foretaste of life in heaven:

> Sexual desire as a manifestation of God's wisdom has, independently of its manifest function, another function: when the individual yields to it, he experiences a delight which would be without match if it were lasting. It is the foretaste of the delights secured for men in Paradise, because to make a promise to men of delights they have not tasted before would be ineffective. This earthly delight, imperfect because limited in time, is a powerful motivation to incite men to try and attain the perfect delight, the eternal delight and therefore urges men to adore God so as to reach heaven. (Gazali, see Mernissi, 1985).

Female sexuality

In Islam, female sexuality is described in positive terms. Importance is placed on a woman's active participation in the sexual act and her right to sexual gratification. Gazali describes men and women as cooperating partners in pleasure. Women, he says, also 'release sperm'. This is strikingly different to Christian thought of that time. St Thomas Aquinas (1224–1274), more than a century after Gazali, held that women did not have the same sexual needs as men because their sexuality was 'cold'. This 'coldness' came from women's inability to produce sperm. Instead of sperm, said Aquinas, women could only produce a defective waste product – menstrual blood (Guneng, 1987).

In Islam, women have the same sexual needs as men which must be satisfied. Muhammed says: 'Do not satisfy your needs with your wife or concubine like an animal, before you have affectionately spoken with her, pleased and caressed her and before she has satisfied her need with you' (Gazali, see Müftüoglu, 1981). This point is frequently made in defence of the rights Islam has provided to women. The fact that Islam accepts female sexuality as a positive attribute does not mean that it has allowed women to choose an alternative existence, independent from the sexual needs of men. Acknowledgement of women's sexual rights has proceeded side-by-side with a limitation and structuring of the conditions under which women may enjoy their sexuality, and a confinement of women within their sexual role. Islam, with its more indirect, refined and rational approach, subjugates women's sexuality much more effectively than any other ideological system.

The danger in woman

According to some authors, Islam considers the sexual needs of women to be stronger than those of men. This is a central concept that can partially explain the reasoning behind the magnitude of the restrictions placed on the autonomy of women. Mernissi (1985) gives an excellent account of the reasoning behind this attitude. Relying mostly on the works of Gazali, she explains that in Islam woman is not viewed as an inherently weak creature, but she is considered dangerous sexually and otherwise. Mernissi alludes to the word *fitna* which in Arabic means both 'beautiful woman' and 'chaos'. She analyses the implications of that duality, convincingly arguing that in Islam there is an inherent fear of women. The paradox in Islam is not within the individual; it is not between flesh and spirit, or good and evil; it is between male and female.

Woman is considered an active and strong creature. She may not, however, rule over man. To let women rule would be to challenge the intention of God:

> Men have authority over women because God has made the one superior to the others, and because they spend their wealth to maintain them. Good women are obedient. They guard their unseen parts because God has guarded them. As for those from whom you fear disobedience, admonish them and send them to beds apart and beat them. Then if they obey you, take no further action against them. (Koran 4:34; Dawood, 1974)

This verse is like a declaration of war against 'disobedient' women. Nothing is said about why God has designed men to spend their wealth on maintaining women, however the necessity for women to obey is underlined, together with men's right to punish. Islam is very strict in this matter: women shall not have authority over men under any circumstances. Gazali quotes from the Prophet: 'There is no salvation for a man or a nation who allows woman to rule over them. They will be devastated.' The reason why the Koran and the Prophet make these very definite statements, according to many Muslim feminists, is a deeply rooted conviction that women's power, if uncontrolled, will bring chaos to the brotherhood of men. Islam represented the final victory of patriarchy over any remaining woman-centred cults and beliefs of earlier times. In Islam, women were not to be allowed to have any authority in society other than in their capacity of servicing, and becoming extensions of, men – as wives or mothers.

Women must be controlled

The dogma that is so positive, with respect to the biological potential of the genders, makes a sudden turn and becomes prohibitive. Men and women must know their place in the social order. There is a conflict of power between the genders and men must not give women the opportunity to take the upper hand. Men must dominate: 'God has created man master over woman. Men who do not dominate women dispute God and follow Satan' (Gazali, see Müftüoglu, 1981).

Christian clergy in the Middle Ages believed that collaboration with Satan was possible for human beings, particularly for women, a fact that led to the disastrous witch hunts. The above quotation from Gazali, when interpreted with the Islamic version of the original sin in which responsibility is not only placed on women, has interesting implications: men are considered to be collaborators of Satan if they do not dominate women.

Men bear the mission of God on Earth: they stand next to God. Muhammed states: 'If I were to advise anybody to worship anything other than God, I would advise women to worship their husbands.' In Christianity, women earn the grace of God by remaining celibate. In Islam, women earn God's grace by obeying their husbands: 'The woman who dies with her husband's blessings shall be admitted to paradise' (Gazali, see Müftüoglu, 1981). Not only shall women be obedient, but they must also be grateful. Muhammed recounts a dream he had: "I dreamt of hell. Most persons burning in the flames were women." "Why was that so, oh Prophet?" "Because they are ungrateful and often curse their husbands."

Absolute gender roles

The message on gender roles is clear: men dominate, women obey. Prescriptions for social conduct, physical appearance and gender segregation are also well-defined. Neither can imitate or take over the role of the other: 'Damned be the woman who tries to be like a man. Damned be the man who imitates woman' (Gazali, see Müftüoglu, 1981).

Each gender must be the antithesis of the other. Muhammed's son-in-law, Ali, one of the most authoritative figures in Islam, prescribes that while men should be generous, women should be thrifty, so that they can protect their husband's possessions; while men should be affectionate, women should be callous, so they do not show appreciation to any other than their husbands; and while men should be brave, good women should be cowards, so they mistrust the world and do not dare to leave the security of their homes (Gazali, see Müftüoglu, 1981).

Islam's firm insistence on moulding the personalities of men and women in opposite poles, reflects the need of a patriarchy to protect itself from some imagined threats from women. 'Be careful about the rights of women,' said Muhammed on his deathbed, 'for they are prisoners at your hands.' The phrase conjures the image of a war between genders, with women being taken as prisoners, by men.

Male jealousy

A Muslim man is expected to control women through what is called a 'natural jealousy' given to men by God. Muhammed says: 'Be jealous of your women and protect them, as God is jealous of you and protects you.' In another Hadis, he is quoted as saying:

> 'There are three groups of people who shall not be allowed into paradise: masculinized women, alcoholics and *deyyuses*.' The congregation then asks, 'What is a deyyus, o prophet?' to which he answers, 'A deyyus is a man who feels no jealously for his daughter, wife, mother or sister'. (Gazali, see Müftüoglu, 1981)

This humiliating term refers to men who do not control their women: a deyyus is a man with no pride and principles, no honour. In order for a man to be respected in society, his unmarried daughters and sisters must be virgins. His wife, mother, sisters and daughters must not engage in extramarital relations. An honourable man must keep an eagle-eye on the actions of women.

But this is easier said than done in Islam where conventions on gender relations are established in accordance with the maxim: 'If something is possible, it is probable' (Demircan, 1985). The reasoning is as follows: 'if the physical appearance of a woman can awaken sexual feelings in a man, even though she is not aware of it, this will probably lead him to want her, which may lead to adultery.' Thus women must be covered so that no one can see their bodies. Or, to give another example: 'If the warmth of a woman's hand can excite an unrelated man, this may lead to illicit flirting and would endanger the woman's chastity.' Thus, men and women should not shake hands. This line of thinking can be carried to absurd degrees, to the extent of prohibiting even the most innocent human interaction between the genders, including prohibition of any asexual aspirations a woman may have, such as listening to music in the company of men, or getting an education or gaining outside employment. The education of women is particularly problematic: 'if education is going to lead to employment, and if the place of employment is sexually desegregated, then men will see our women and this will awaken their lust. This will threaten their chastity and we may lose our honour.' This thinking obliges men to feel a paranoid responsibility for their women because the actions of women define their moral integrity.

The honour ethic

The strong need to control women can be traced to a phenomenon which is older than Islam, the honour ethic. This is based on the belief that women cannot be trusted to protect their chastity in the best interests of the patriarchal society. This duty is given to the male relatives of women. An honourable man is someone who has moral qualities such as honesty, not stealing another's possessions, etc., and whose women kin remain chaste. If the sexuality of a woman is violated against the wishes of the men in her family, the men lose their honour: they become deyyuses or cuckolds. In order to be respected in society, men must have honour and women must have shame. A woman affiliated to a man helps him maintain his honour by her own feelings of shame that lead her to behave discreetly and to confine herself to serving her family (Sachs, 1984; Peristiany, 1965; Aronowitz, 1988).

The honour ethic as it applies to women's sexuality is not specific to Islam, but exists in many other non-Muslim societies. A man's honour was closely related to the behaviour of his female kin in Northern Europe until recently, although the concept has now become obsolete (Sachs, 1984). This ethic, however, is still deeply entrenched in most Christian Mediterranean societies, and is often described as the most important factor in the subordination of women throughout the region (Peristiany, 1965; Safilios-Rothschild, 1969; Quastana and Casanova, 1986; Dodd, 1973). Thus the sexuality of women is subject to as stringent a control, and men feel as strongly dishonoured by the loss of their women's chastity, among non-Muslim populations in the area. Islamic teaching on the natural jealousy of men and the necessity to control women actually overlaps with the honour ethic, strengthening and structuring it. As in other Mediterranean societies, even when people distance themselves from formal religiosity, the honour ethic, in respect of the sexuality of women, persists. It remains the most sacred convention guiding family organization and gender relations in Turkey (Magnarella, 1974; Kagitcibasi, 1981), including the non-Muslim minorities such as the Jews, Armenians, Assyrians and Greeks.

The failure of women to remain chaste – including cases of rape – is a social catastrophe of the highest order as it brings shame to the whole family. It is a disgrace which is so difficult to repair that sometimes the vengeance for lost honour may include drastic measures, causing bloodshed and feuds. Because the loss of honour brings such great grief, it is considered very important to take all possible precautions to avoid anything that may threaten a woman's chastity. Hence 'good' women must tolerate the domination of men to preserve the family's honour.

It would not be possible to encourage women to accept unconditional obedience if they did not receive something in exchange. In societies that place a high value on the chastity of women, obedient women are, in fact, accorded the greatest degree of respect. A woman who sacrifices personal goals in order to obey a difficult father, and later a jealous husband, and brings up several well-adjusted children, often commands more respect than an unmarried woman who rejects male control, even if she were to make a vitally important scientific invention. Women recognize that challenging the honour ethic will bring a loss of social respectability and they, therefore, generally respect it as strongly as do men.

The degree of internalization of the honour ethic by women in Turkish society is exemplified in a study on patterns of homicide. A study carried out by Özgur and Sunar in 1982 shows that the defence of honour is the normatively approved motive for the most violent measure – homicide – by both men and women, and that women are twice as likely as men to commit this crime in order to protect their chastity. The following is an example of the extent to which Turkish women sometimes go in the pursuance of honour:

> A woman is sitting in a prison outside Istanbul with her child. She is there because she killed her husband. She killed her husband because he failed to assert his honour.
>
> The woman became attached to and had a relationship with another man during her husband's long stay in Germany as an immigrant worker. Her husband found out about the affair when he suddenly came home and caught her with her lover. He reproached his wife and did not want to see her, but after a while he took her back and they began living together as if nothing had happened.
>
> The woman waited everyday that her husband would punish her. But the husband did not do anything and did not show any signs of wanting to take revenge. After some weeks the woman became desperate. To not be punished for what she had done was a greater shame for her than punishment. The only way her husband could regain his honour in his society was that he would die. She killed him.
>
> Now she sits in prison and waits for the punishment society will give her for her crime. A crime of this type receives milder judgement because it

concerns honour. The woman says, 'I wanted to save my husband's honour'. (From *Cumhuriyet*, a Turkish newspaper, 19 July 1978; see Sachs, 1984).

Turkish women are socialized into considering male honour as being integral to their own. They do not want to jeopardize the respectability they gain when they are attached to honourable men, even if they sometimes pay a very high price for it. It is difficult to judge the point where Islamic teaching on the necessity to control women ceases and the cross-cultural honour ethic exerts its influence. There is no doubt, however, that the honour ethic is a deeply ingrained convention, with which women must somehow come to terms. Further examples of how the ethic moulds the behaviour of people in Turkish society appear in the following chapters.

3. Turkish Women Today

The Republican era can roughly be divided into two periods. The years from 1923 up to the 1950s constitute the Kemalist era, ruled by a single-party regime under Ataturk (1881–1938) or his close associates. Although a few attempts at democracy were made during this period, all opposition that emerged – whether liberal, fundamentalist or Marxist – was promptly suppressed as it conflicted with Kemalist plans for Westernization and industrialization under state control. Kemalists had chosen capitalism as the economic system, although they were cautious of a fully market-driven economy. They were also staunchly determined not to allow religious or class rule.

The issue of women was given priority by Kemalists (Tekeli, 1982) because the dogmatism in Islamic law, and particularly its approach to women, did not allow a transformation of society into a Western model. The Kemalists opened the way for women's education and participation in public life by legal reforms and coercion.

When declared a Republic, Turkey was an impoverished agricultural country in which 84% of the population lived in rural areas with very poor communications with the rest of the country and virtually none with the outside world. Women had for centuries been living in circumstances described earlier. They had not, to any appreciable degree, demanded rights equal to those of men. The educational level was extremely low: only about 5% of women were literate. Even fewer women were wage earners. It is, therefore, not surprising that when the new civil code was enacted in 1929, only a minority of urban upper class women were able to take advantage of the legal changes mandating their emancipation (Abadan-Unat, 1986).

There was intensive publicity about the new rights given to women. Kemalists held the Ottoman centuries of Islamic law responsible for all the injustices women had experienced. A main Kemalist theme was that the brave and self-sacrificing Turkish women, who had contributed to victory in war and the independence of the Republic, had been granted the rights they deserved. Women were now working, it was said, side-by-side with men, rebuilding a proud, civilized and independent country (Afetinan, 1982). Many people sincerely believed that gender equality had been achieved through these reforms. They did not question the traditional role of women (Özbay, 1986).

Turkey did not enter World War II, maintaining a precarious position of non-alignment. This threatened to isolate the country from the Allies at the end of the war and encouraged the Soviets to demand military bases on Turkish territory when the war was over. In order to break the isolation, protect itself against Soviet interests outside and socialist developments inside the country, and also to be included among the countries that would be assisted by the Truman Doctrine and the Marshall Plan, Turkey felt obliged to assure Western powers of its loyalty and signed the United Nations convention soon after its inception.

By that time, the single-party regime that had ruled the country for more than two decades was being criticized both internally and externally as being anti-democratic. In 1946, an attempt at multi-party democracy was made, including the liberal Democrat Party as well as a number of Marxist parties. Following the suppression of the Marxist parties, the Democrat Party assumed the role of main opposition.

A turning point in modern Turkish history occurred in the elections of 1950 when the Democrat Party was victorious by a dramatic margin. Soon afterwards, Turkey sent troops to the Korean War and entered the North Atlantic Treaty Organization (NATO). Government policies from that time on were to lead to significant changes in Turkey: increased political, economic and military dependence on the United States; integration into the world market; and the development of a liberal capitalist economy.

The Democrat Party revoked many of Atatürk's social reforms and opened the state-controlled economy to the free market. The economy was grossly mismanaged, leading to a huge deficit in the balance of payments and high inflation by the end of the 1950s. This was accompanied by a forced devaluation and stabilization programme. To counter criticism, the Democrats resorted to repressive, unconstitutional tactics against the opposition.

The Democrat Party government was overthrown by a military coup in 1960, following increasing dissent and further repression by the government. Subsequent trials of government officials accused of violating the constitution resulted in the execution of three Democrat Party leaders and prison sentences for 433 others. During the 17-month military rule, voters approved in a referendum Turkey's first liberal–democratic constitution which enabled people to experience, for about a decade, an exciting period of freedom of expression and assembly. Noteworthy events during the 1960s included the beginnings of labour union struggles, the establishment of a variety of political parties, the awakening of anti-imperialist sentiments and increased radicalization of intellectuals and students.

These developments were halted by a new military coup in 1971. The military charged that the government had led the country to 'anarchy, fratricidal strife and social and economic unrest' and forced a change of prime ministers. Martial law was instituted and brutal repression of democratic freedoms followed. In response to the repression, a left-of-centre social democratic movement, as well as fascist and fundamentalist movements, developed. Political polarization intensified during the following years as the economy deteriorated. A series of civilian coalition governments was either unable or unwilling to halt public unrest. By 1979, Turkey was on the brink of civil war.

A third military coup in 1980 brought with it even more stringent suppression of democratic rights and a new conservative constitution, before the government was once more returned to civilians. As Turkish society today undergoes rapid social transformation, the struggle for democracy, social and economic justice and human rights is continuing at all levels. Restrictions and violations of basic democratic freedoms still exist.

The official perspective on the status of women in Turkey is that of the Kemalists: gender equality of opportunity is guaranteed by law. According to this approach, women who take advantage of legal changes are emancipated: women are not oppressed in society unless they choose to allow themselves to be oppressed.

Parallel to the Islamic awakening on the Arabian Peninsula, and the fundamentalist take-over in Iran, movements advocating a return to the Islamic, religious way of life are gaining strength in Turkey. They are often supported by right-wing powers. Fundamentalists summarily reject Kemalist ideology and the goal of Westernization. They criticize Western influence on society as morally corrupting and an enslavement of Muslims by a power other than God. The issue of the status of women is central to fundamentalism. They argue that Islam provides respect and protection for women. They assert that the 'new' women who strive for the rights and liberties attained by their sisters in Western societies risk becoming the playthings of men and the slaves of wage-labour. Women should remain in the private domain and let their men provide for them, they say. Unlike earlier periods in Republican history, small but significant numbers of young educated women are now joining the ranks of fundamentalists and, as such, the movement must be reckoned with by feminists.

Marxists are undertaking a re-evaluation of Turkish history, particularly Kemalism, and criticize both Kemalist and fundamentalist views of women. They explain the subordination of women as a class issue and argue that the subordination of women will end when the system of production is changed.

Thus, as in the Tanzimat period, there is agreement that the issue of the status of women is a national concern. But the problem, it is believed, is limited to certain groups. Kemalists believe that less educated peasant women are restrained by religion and tradition from exercising the rights available to them. Kemalists place the blame on traditional women. For fundamentalists, 'liberated' and thus 'immoral' women who reject the premises of the protective Islamic patriarchy are the problem and the blame is put on Westernization. For Marxists, it is the women who do not join in the struggle for a social and economic transformation of society who are the problem; blame is placed on 'parasitic' women who depend on men, instead of struggling to create a socialist state.

Since the 1980s, however, there has been a new awareness that women, regardless of social background, education and ideology, share common problems by virtue of their gender. The increase in academic studies about women in Turkey has contributed to this awareness. Modern studies began with monographs of the 1940s which described the villages studied as not having been reached by Kemalist reforms. These monographs showed that peasant women were subordinate to men and were beasts of burden in the hierarchic and segregated patriarchal family, whose existence was still defined according to the Islamic–Anatolian tradition. The only power women ever exercised was in their role as mothers. When peasants began migrating to the cities during the 1950s, Kemalist city-dwellers also realized that the status of many Turkish women was not as it was being taught in the schools. In the 1960s a series of fertility studies further enhanced the knowledge of gender relations in Turkey. These studies showed that not only the peasants, but also the small town and city women, were subordinated in a system espousing patriarchal values.

The United Nations Decade for Women (1975–1985) was an opportunity to concentrate on women's issues. There was an increase in translations of feminist classics; but perhaps more important, studies were made of women by women within the country (Kagitcibasi, 1981; Timur, 1978; Tekeli, 1982) which contributed to the realization of how widespread and unquestioned was male dominance at all levels of society (Özbay, 1986).

The growing awareness was not only a social science experience. Some educated women, many with roots in the Marxist or radical student movements of the 1960s and 1970s, others raised in the Kemalist or Islamic traditions, also began voicing their disillusionment. They felt they were not free and did not have equal rights or opportunities in a society that moulded their existence according to male, patriarchal needs and limited their prospects for human growth. During the last decade an independent women's movement has been taking shape in Turkey. At the present time there are feminist organizations in most major cities. These groups are still small and their participants are generally professional urban women, but they are a highly vocal group who have been able to engender debates. They seem to be determined to question the nature of male dominance and female submission. The question of women continues to be a burning issue in Turkey (Tekeli, 1986).

The Legal Status of Women

Women have legal rights equal to men with some exceptions. The civil code which was adapted from the code of Switzerland, gives equal rights to women in matters relating to marriage, divorce, custody of children, legal testimony and inheritance. Within marriage the code stipulates that the husband is the head of the family. The husband represents the union and the wife and children carry his family name. The husband has the right to choose the family residence and may prohibit his wife from seeking employment outside their home if he believes this will hinder her responsibilities in the home (Abadan-Unat, 1986).

Divorce is made easy. Incompatibility is accepted as grounds for termination of marriage. The needy spouse may demand alimony for up to one year following the divorce, but only on the condition the needy partner is not at fault for the dissolution of the union.

The establishment of brothels is allowed, under the supervision of the ministries of health and the interior, in contradiction to the penal code which prohibits the encouragement of prostitution. A paragraph in the penal code reduces the sentence for rape or abduction by two-thirds if a female victim is a prostitute. Abortion upon request, originally prohibited in the penal code, has been allowed since 1983. If the woman is married, her husband's consent is required (Abadan-Unat, 1986).

There are special provisions in the labour code for employed women which stipulate maternity leave as six weeks prior to and six weeks following delivery. Upon returning to her job a mother is allowed two half-hour periods per day for breast-feeding. The code prohibits the employment of women in mines, laying cables, construction of sewage tunnels and all other jobs involving underground work. Women are also prohibited from working on night shift in industrial jobs (Kaplan, 1985).

There is no national social insurance in Turkey. The three social security schemes that exist cover only formally employed people and their dependents who constitute about 10% of the total population.

Legal rights, however, are not meaningful in a society where women are stigmatized if by taking full advantage of their rights they threaten to violate moral norms and family conventions (Youssef, 1974, Bingöllu-Sayari, 1979). The strongest convention defining women's rights in Turkey is not in the laws of the land, but in the collective subconscious which is defined by Islam and the honour ethic.

Family Formations and Lifestyles

Turkey is a country with striking class differences. Below, a general account of lifestyles according to place of residence, which to a large extent defines social class, is given. It should be kept in mind that generalizations are impossible to avoid and Turkish society is more heterogeneous than the account may suggest.

The village women
Until quite recently, village life was held as the norm in defining the values of Turkish families and the status of women. The majority of the Turkish population have their immediate roots in a village. Modifications to lifestyles which occurred as a result of rural to urban migration will be discussed later.

The average peasant woman gets married soon after puberty, at around 15 to 17 years of age. Village women do not have to worry about finding a spouse: they are assisted in that effort by their families and the community. By the age of 20 almost all women are married and have borne children. Marriages are arranged for girls at a young age primarily because of the needs of agriculture and human reproductive factors. It is thought these functions can be fully performed from the onset of puberty. Boys are also married at a young age. This practice is supported by Islamic dogma which bans celibacy as well as premarital relations; sexual needs must be gratified when they are manifest, and this must occur within marriage.

Over two-thirds of all marriages in Turkey are arranged. In villages an arranged marriage is the norm. A match is sometimes determined prior to the child reaching puberty, and 36% of such marriages are between first cousins or more distant relatives (Timur, 1979). In arranging marriages, families take into consideration factors such as strengthening economic bonds between two families and whether a marriage would contribute to the highest possible living standard for their child. The reason for the high frequency of marriages to kin is the desire to enhance the concentration of property, power and solidarity within the larger family.

Whether the boy and girl are compatible or in love are not primary considerations, as marriage in most parts of Turkish society is not considered a private affair. It is primarily an economic necessity and a social–religious duty. Some consideration may be given to the romantic feelings of the boy, but such feelings are considered inappropriate for girls and rarely are given much weight. Some Turkish proverbs repudiate the choice of spouse made by girls: 'If you let a girl have her way, she will choose either the drum player or the flute player.'

The process of arranging a marriage, whether in a village or an urban area, usually begins with the initiative of a son who tells his mother of his desire to get married. If the boy is slow to make that decision, his family may decide the time has come for his marriage. If it has not been decided beforehand, the boy may suggest a girl's name. The boy's mother and some of his other older female relatives then pay a first visit to the chosen girl's mother. During that visit the girl is seen briefly, but she does not participate in the meeting. The possibility of marriage is informally discussed among the women. If all goes well, the chosen girl's mother assumes responsibility for informing her daughter and husband that there is a suitor. The girl may at this stage offer her opinion of the potential mate. Her consent of course helps, but a girl may be offered in marriage even if she doesn't agree with the match. In one study 11% of all women were found to have been married against their will (Timur, 1979). The final word lies with the girl's father. The family would usually be reluctant to force a daughter into marriage, primarily to ensure her happiness but also because forcing her would be to risk the possibility of her elopement with another boy, threatening family honour.

Assuming the girl concurs with the choice, a second meeting is held, this time at the boy's home, which the two fathers attend. The desirability of marriage, followed by a discussion of practical matters, such as the bride-price, the size of the trousseau, mutual responsibilities and the date of the wedding are agreed upon. The decision is then announced at an engagement ceremony, rings are exchanged and wedding preparations begin.

Romance between future spouses is not of primary importance. Most marriages are entered into with very little knowledge of the mate's personality. In a village, the couple would know about one another's appearance and reputation. They would have played and gone to school together during early childhood, but would scarcely have had any private contact since then. Any type of premarital relation, be this as innocent as taking a walk, is considered improper.

It is sometimes possible to flirt and pass secret messages. In such a case the boy would usually ask for the girl's hand. He might be turned down because the girl's family has other plans for her, or he cannot afford the bride price. If the boy's desire to marry the girl is strong enough, he might take the drastic measure of abducting her; or they might agree on elopement if their feelings are mutual. The girl is either kidnapped or agrees to run away from her parental home and spends a couple of nights with the boy. In either case virginity is lost and marriage becomes a *de facto* obligation without the necessity of paying a bride price. Abduction or elopement with a girl is risky business, punishable by law as rape. In some regions of Turkey it can also lead to blood feuds to avenge the loss of family honour. Despite these risks, about 10% of all marriages in Turkey are initiated this way (Timur, 1978). Most families try to make arrangements for a peaceful union.

The bride-price (*bashlik*), the payment the boy's family makes for the girl, corresponds to the mehir prescribed in Islam. It has been customary in Anatolia since the Hittite period. It was also widespread among Turks before their conversion to Islam. The payment is compensation made to the girl's family for the loss of her labour. It also provides for the bride's trousseau and gives her a degree of financial security. A bride-price is paid in about half of all marriages in Turkey (Timur, 1979). In villages it is the norm.

The amount of bride-price varies. It can be expensive. Contrary to what the Koran stipulates, in Turkey the payment is not made to the girl but to her father, who then decides how it will be distributed. Usually, the family takes about one-third, spends another third on the trousseau and converts the rest into gold which is given to the daughter as jewellery. Gold is popular because its value rises with inflation and it can easily be converted into cash in case of emergency. A bride would get more gold, as gifts from relatives, at the time of the wedding. Gold and clothing are usually the only property a peasant woman has unless her husband dies before she does. Again, contrary to Islam which gives women the right to inherit half as much as male heirs, and the Turkish civil code which gives women equal inheritance rights, many peasant women are compelled by their families at the time of marriage to transfer their inheritance rights to their brothers 'for the sake of family unity' (Magnarella, 1979).

Dugun means wedding in Turkish. The word is derived from a verb meaning 'to tie', and, as such, refers to the binding together of two people. Weddings are one of the high points in village life and consist of two ceremonies: one conducted at the girl's and the other at the boy's paternal home. Ceremonies differ in various regions, but each generally symbolizes the girl's farewell to her parental home and her acceptance into the *el* (foreign) family. Before the wedding day the girl and boy have separate parties with friends and relatives of their own sex. On the wedding day, the groom and guests dress up and go to the girl's home. They are invited for refreshments and later witness the first wedding ceremony. The ceremonies may be civil, religious or both. Because religious marriages are no longer recognized under Turkish law, most families now insist on civil ceremonies.

The girl is then taken to the door where she kisses the hands of her elders. She then leaves for her husband's home, where she is taken in by her in-laws in a second ceremony. From that moment on she will belong to that household. More entertaining follows. Then the bride is taken to her room. A female relative of the groom accompanies her to help with her clothing and to talk to her and ease the tension. A little later, the groom is pushed into this room by his friends with much back-slapping and laughter.

Considering the large body of anecdotal evidence, this first nuptial night may be one of the most traumatic experiences in the lives of many people. Women enter marriage at a very young age, as virgins. Although most peasant girls are somewhat knowledgeable about the mechanics of sex, their information is fragmentary, based on observing animals or eavesdropping on conversations between older women (peasant women are quite explicit in discussing sexuality among themselves). The boy may have visited the town brothel, but his knowledge is usually not significantly more sophisticated than the bride's. This is the first time they find themselves alone in a room with an unrelated person of the opposite sex, about whom they know little. In spite of this, the youths are expected to perform sex immediately, or at least during the course of the night, by the crowd waiting outside which is singing, dancing and shooting guns in the air. Evidence of performance must be produced before the bride's mother-in-law sends the guests home and goes to bed herself. The evidence is a piece of bedsheet or a handkerchief stained with virginal blood. Failure to present this soon enough would cast shadows over the boy's virility or the girl's chastity, with serious consequences for the honour of their families.

The first years with her husband's family are usually the most difficult period in a peasant woman's life. Although the majority of households (73%) in Turkey are nuclear, many newly wed couples live with the groom's family for a few years before they establish their own household. Couples often live in very close proximity to the groom's family. Relations between related households are very intense, similar to extended family relations except that each family has a separate roof over its head.

The bride is referred to as a *gelin*. This word means 'the one who came', suggesting that she is considered an outsider. A young gelin is usually at the bottom of the family hierarchy. Under the scrutinizing supervision of her mother-in-law, she is trained to adjust to the new household by doing exactly as she is told, learning to be skilful, obedient, quick and hard-working. She may be punished by almost anyone in the house. She does not find understanding or support in her husband either; his loyalty to his mother and family is usually stronger than that to her. Generally, public displays of affection between husband and wife are frowned upon. In some regions of Turkey, the *gelin* is not allowed to speak in the presence of the father-in-law. She may publicly address others, including her husband, only when there is an urgent need.

A gelin is expected to work and serve, be modest and shy, keep quiet and produce children. Her situation improves somewhat when she gives birth, but she is not accepted as a true member of the family until she has borne a son. The three greatest catastrophes for many Turkish women are not proving their virginity at marriage, sterility and not being able to produce a son. These are conditions that legitimize divorce. In rural areas where divorce rates are extremely low, sterility may lead to the remarriage of the husband, by religious ceremony, to another woman (the *kuma*).

The work load of women in a village is heavy. In 1985, 85% of the total female labour force of 7.6 million (1985) was engaged in agriculture (Table 3.1). This type of production requires minimal qualifications; possessing an education which may qualify a woman for some other type of task tends to remove her from all income-earning activities (Özbay, 1982).

Normally, girls do not receive as much schooling as boys. The compulsory education is five years. As shown in Table 3.2, almost seven decades after the formation of the Republic, 32% of all women are still illiterate compared to 13% of men. The rates are higher when only village populations are considered.

Table 3.1. Distribution of the economically active population (over 12 years of age) according to occupation (%), 1985

Occupation	Men	Women
Professional, administrative	6	4
Clerical, sales, services	18	5
Agriculture	40	85
Industry	30	2
Total (millions)	13.9	7.6

Source: Turkish State Board of Statistics, 1988

Table 3.2. Educational status of those over 6 years of age, 1985, percentage

Years of school	Men	Women
Illiterate	13	32
1–4	19	18
5	48	39
6–8	8	4
9–11	8	5
>12	3	1
Other	1	1
Total (millions)	21.8	21.3

Source: Turkish State Board of Statistics, 1988

Not all villages have school facilities, which explains a portion of the illiteracy. The most significant reason why girls are kept from pursuing an education is the belief that it is not necessary for them. Sending rural children to school means allowing them to take time from productive work. In a country where agriculture, food production and preservation, animal husbandry and similar activities are still carried out manually mainly by women, only those children who are expected to make a greater contribution to the family at a later time may be allowed to avoid the immediate needs of the farm. These are the boys. It is believed that there is no point in making educational investments in girls who will join the labour force of some other family when they grow up.

Agricultural work is seasonal, involving intensive work for every available able-bodied person from early spring until autumn. Women's involvement in agriculture is greater than that of men. Because Turkish agriculture is under-mechanized, most work on small- to medium-sized landholdings is still carried out manually, sometimes with tools that date back to the time of the Hittites. Men do those tasks that require greater physical strength, such as using the plough and threshing a harvest, or the easiest tasks, such as using the more sophisticated tools and machines. Most intermediate tasks, which are the most time consuming, such as sowing, weeding, reaping, picking and transporting, are carried out by women and children. In families where the men seek summer employment away from the farms or have migrated to Europe, women also do the heavier tasks. Raising vegetables and tending animals are exclusively female and children's tasks. Only 2% of the army of working women are salaried; the rest are unsalaried family workers who, in season, work around the clock. In addition to the outdoor activity, women are also responsible for the housework which includes preserving and storing up to 60% of the food supply for the winter as well as tasks such as weaving carpets, sewing the family's clothes and taking care of the younger children and any disabled family members.

An off-season day, when a peasant woman does not need to work in the fields, is described in an anthropological study as follows:

A woman gets up before sunrise. First she starts a fire and kneads the *bazlama* (a type of bread) dough which takes two hours to ferment. In the meantime she puts the soup to cook and goes down to the stable. She milks the cow and sheep – she wakes one of the children to hold the head of the animals. Then she carries water from the village fountain. She takes the soup, which is ready by now, from the fire and puts on the milk to boil. When the milk is boiled, she puts on the bazlama. She wakes the father and the children. Breakfast is eaten: it is cleared away, the mattresses are rolled up and put away in the bedding closet. She sees off the father . . . After putting out the cows and the sheep to pasture, she cleans the stable. She mixes cattle dung with hay and sticks it on the wall to dry for making *tezek* to be used as fuel. She washes the breakfast dishes and very quickly churns the yogurt that was set to ferment the night before, putting the buttermilk in the bag and the butter in a jar. She feeds the chickens, sends the boy to take out the ox or to collect pine cones. She herself goes to the vegetable garden with her daughter. The work in the garden, such as weeding, hoeing, opening up the sluices, etc., continues until noon. When she returns home she packs a food basket for her husband (if he is in the fields or the woods), and she eats whatever she finds. The house is swept and cleaned. Soon preparations for supper begin. At sunset the sheep and cattle return home. She looks for those that may be missing. Those animals that have followed the animals of others are collected and put in the stable. The father is helped with his cart on his return. His cart is unloaded and the oxen or horses are put in the stable. The cows and sheep are fed and milked again. The cream of the milk is separated. The milk is put to boil and the starter put to make yogurt. Supper is eaten, dishes cleared and washed. The children begin getting sleepy by the last mouthfuls. The mother sweeps the floor, spreads out the mattresses, undresses the children and puts them to bed. If the children's clothes need mending, this is done immediately so that the torn/unstitched parts do not grow larger. After some more tidying here and there, she listens to the animals in the stable to hear if there is any coughing, moaning or sounds of their giving birth. And after saying all the prayers accumulated during the day, she gains the right to go to bed, ready to wake up with the sound of a moaning sheep giving birth. The mother does the entire work with the help of her children. Work in a childless home is hard and takes a long time to finish. (Balaman, 1985)

Women, however, do not consider themselves working people. If one asks a peasant man what he does, he would say he is a farmer. A woman would answer the same question by saying 'I sit at home', in spite of the fact that she carries the brunt of farming activities plus all housework, rarely having any time to just 'sit'.

One reason women's work is not acknowledged is because in the villages their contribution is unpaid family labour. Even though it generates income, the final cash is collected and brought home by men. The other reason is that social values ascribe the breadwinner role to men. Not allowing women to work for an income and not using women's property is a matter of honour. Internalized as this value is, not even women themselves are ready to admit that they are contributing, with their labour, to the financial well-being of their families. They see their daily activities as a natural component of their duties as wife and mother. The ideal is to be a housewife, not to work for an income. Many women say with pride, 'My husband does not allow me to work.' As soon as the family gains some financial security, women are commonly withdrawn from production. The 2% of women who work for wages in large agricultural enterprises come from poor families and are pitied.

Most peasant women have no personal income, very little property and no old-age security. This renders them very dependent on their families. They depend on their husband and his family for their immediate, day-to-day survival. They depend on the help of their children to survive the workload. They depend on their sons for survival in old age. It is thus important for a woman to have children, particularly boys. If forced to make a choice, 84% of people in Turkey would say they prefer sons over daughters, mainly because of the economic input of boys (Kagitcibasi, 1981). The labour contribution girls make prior to their marriage is overlooked. At the age of 15 to 17, girls will leave home to join the labour pool of another family. Sons will remain, bring in their brides, reproduce, help out day-to-day and take care of their parents when they are old.

The average fertility rate of married women in Turkey is 5.15. Fertility rates are higher for rural women who, by the time they reach their late forties, would have experienced an average of six pregnancies and borne five children, of whom four would have survived (Hacettepe University, 1989). Because of the high infant and child mortality rates women fall pregnant more frequently than they otherwise might to ensure the survival of some offspring and that at least one son reaches maturity. This takes its toll on their health: the maternal mortality rate in Turkey is about fifty times as high as in Sweden (Table 3.3).

The birth of a son brings much joy. The mother of several sons is a proud woman. When she reaches her late thirties, these boys will bring home brides and she will reach the apex of her life, exercising power over the labour of the brides and the minds and hearts of her sons. She gradually retires from the heavy work to the role of a supervising mother-in-law. The birth of a daughter is not appreciated unless there are already sons in the family. A woman who has only daughters feels embarrassment. At the birth of another daughter the woman is thought to have brought misfortune to the family. She is urged to bear children until she has a son. In eastern regions of Turkey, daughters are not even regarded as offspring; when asked how many children he has, a father would give only the number of his sons. Even the tradition of allowing mothers who have just delivered to rest with their infants for 40 days may not be followed if there are too many daughters. After a few weeks, the indignation subsidies as Turkish people are generally fond of all children.

Table 3.3. Maternal and child mortality rates in Turkey and Sweden, 1986

Country	Maternal mortality[1]	0–5 year child mortality[2]
Turkey	207	99
Sweden	4	7

[1] Per 100,000 live births
[2] Per 1000

Source: State of the World's Children, UNICEF, 1989

For most village women, the first 40 days after delivery (known as the *lohusa* period) is the only time they have the opportunity to attend solely to their children. Thereafter, they will have to resume all their other responsibilities and children are cared for alongside other activities. When a mother is too busy, older siblings, women relatives, neighbours or grandparents tend the children. The whole village community, whether related or not, takes responsibility for all children.

Children up to the age of six or seven are given complete freedom with very little gender segregation. Everything they do is tolerated with a minimum of punishment. They run around as they wish and people make a genuine effort to admire, please and cuddle them. People make such a fuss over small children, that there has evolved a theory of an 'evil eye', with accompanying magical practices that are believed to protect children (and others) from the effects of too much admiration (Sachs, 1983).

Mothers take primary responsibility for the children when they have time. Fathers do not normally change children's nappies or cut their toenails, but they do play with their children and take them on excursions to nearby villages or to a coffee shop. Children also get much affection and care from their grandparents who normally let their son and the gelin do all the heavy work while they pamper the young ones. The grandmother attends the children, sings, tells stories and teaches them handicrafts. The grandfather takes them with him when going out to graze the cattle or plays hide-and-seek with them while guarding the fields against birds. The attitude towards young children is one of amused affection for their naivety. They are not encouraged to learn concepts and grow up too quickly, as their childhood is short, ending just before puberty.

Most people fondly remember their early childhood, probably because they were pampered so much during this time of their life. Notwithstanding this, Turks generally do not analyse their childhood memories as frequently as do Europeans. To be critical of the treatment they received during early childhood and to blame their 'self-sacrificing' mothers and 'honourable' fathers, as they popularly describe their parents, for the neuroses they might later develop, is very alien to the Turkish way of looking at the process of maturation. Children are brought up to respect older people and to be deeply grateful to their parents, especially their mother. Affection between mother and child is universal but the relationship in Turkey is exceptionally strong. The following excerpt from a letter written by a 24-year-old immigrant man to his mother illustrates the dimensions of mother-worship:

To my dear mother,
My dear mother, the mother of mothers, the queen of mothers, the one and only mother I have, how are you! I hope you are all right. I regret to have caused you to weep in longing when I called you on the telephone the other evening, but, even though I really cannot afford to make telephone calls, the desire to hear your soft voice sometimes becomes irresistible. I pray to God you and father are feeling well. If you should wonder how I am, I would say I am feeling well . . . I must put an end at this time, even though my heart aches for you. I respectfully kiss your skilful and tired hands; I kiss your lovely, soft eyes. Please pray for me, as I pray for the time when I can be with you again, dear Mother. I also kiss my father's hands. (Personal communication, 1984)

The relationship between mother and son is often the strongest either one will ever have with someone of the opposite sex. The relationship between parents and a daughter is bitter-sweet, shadowed by the fact that she will leave home to live with a husband and his family. The attitude of children to their father is gratitude mixed with fearful respect. It infrequently takes the form of resentment, which is not manifested. The relationship with one's father is generally restrained.

Once a child has reached an age when he or she can take orders to perform simple tasks, socialization into gender roles begins. Girls begin helping their mother around the house and boys follow their father. Their responsibilities increase with age, as they learn the patterns of behaviour expected of them. Girls are taught to be obedient, quiet, hard working, skilful, intelligent in a practical sense (but not informed) and, most important of all, chaste. It is not necessary that they be pretty. Beauty can be dangerous for a girl: it may lead to vanity and improper aspirations. Around the age of nine or ten, girls are no longer allowed to have anything to do with boys other than their brothers, and begin wearing unrevealing clothes and head scarves.

Boys are expected to be strong and fearless. As they mature, they are encouraged to become demanding of the womenfolk, and keen to protect the family honour. A boy of ten or eleven can order his mother and other women around the house and keep a sharp eye on his older sisters. He no longer does any 'woman's work' but is waited on. From puberty, he should be virile and easily tempted by the sight of a revealing woman. These boys and girls then get married to one another and the cycle repeats itself.

As mentioned above, romance and companionship are not major features of the relationship between spouses because marriage is seen mainly as a social and economic institution. Although this perception is prevalent in many societies, it is particularly strong in Turkish culture, as suggested in one large nationwide study. When compared with some developing countries in Asia and with the USA, the lowest level of companionship and role-sharing was found in married couples in Turkey (Kagitcibasi, 1986). If at all, romance will develop later in the marriage. The existence of sexual desire between spouses is considered sufficient to make a marriage function happily. Incompatibility of personality or intellectual differences are not considered sufficient reason for dissolving a marriage.

This does not, of course, mean that romance and affection do not exist between couples but they are not publicly manifested. Being affectionate with one's spouse in the presence of others, or expressing one's feelings, is considered very inappropriate. Men are particularly adamant about this matter. They rarely discuss their wives and daughters with others. When they must, it is only for practical or urgent reasons and they feel embarrassed to do so. Normally, a man does not even refer to his wife by her name, or as his wife, but uses the term 'family' in front of others. When addressing each other, men call their wives 'lady' (*hanum*). Women address their husbands as 'lord' (*bey*). Names are not used.

When the exchange of private, affectionate messages is absolutely necessary,

indirect communication methods may be sought. By tradition, women knit their feelings for their beloved on woollen socks: there are a series of abstract, geometrical motifs which signify certain moods in Turkish folklore and a woman knits any number of these on a woollen stocking and sends it to her beloved. He first 'reads' the stocking, then wears it as a token of love from his sweetheart. To ask a wife as simple a question as whether she is pregnant may be a delicate matter necessitating an elegant communication style, such as poetry. These messages were exchanged between a young husband working in Europe and his wife in Turkey (Boratav, 1985):
The husband asks:

Go, my letter, and come back
Bring news from my beloved
We were one, we became two
Find out if we now are three.

And the wife replies:

Your field has not given crop
Toil again when you come.

Men and women rarely need a deep dialogue with one another. The genders are separated from each other at all levels of social interaction. Women work and entertain among themselves, as do the men. They come together as man and wife for purposes of reproducing the labour power of the family and for meals. The harem-*selamlik* system is still operative in the villages and small towns. Men spend virtually all their spare time outside their homes. A man who sits at home with his wife or shows any preference for her over the company of men would be a laughing stock. In their free time men gather together either at a village coffee shop or in the 'guest room' of one of their friends. If there is no place in particular to go, men would still rather stay outside, gathering under the shade of a tree or leaning against a wall, than go home. Families who can afford to have more than one room in their homes design a second room as a guest room where outside men can enter. Unrelated men and women never socialize together: except for small boys and sons, no males join the company of women; only children and old, post-menopausal women may visit in the company of men. Gender segregation is broken only between family members and for joint projects, such as production. For several months during the high season, men and women work together in the fields (Stirling, 1965).

Female relations are hierarchical with the mother-in-law and other older women presiding and the gelin and younger women at the bottom. Women work, control each other, confide intimacies and help each other within this framework. Relationships are intense and the degree of intimacy between women is extensive (Olson, 1985a; Fallers and Fallers, 1976; Stirling, 1965). Women live in a hostile environment in which they are often described in critical terms such as 'spoon saboteurs' (because they eat), 'ash-dumpers' (because they do useless things and create a mess) and 'long in hair, short in mind' (because they are supposedly stupid). Women are not only under constant control, but fear of male retribution is also ever-present, particularly when women are young. These proverbs, which are still popular, are instructive (Balaman, 1985).

A woman should always feel the pain of the stick on her back and the presence of a baby in her belly.

When beating a woman, the colour of the [white] scarf on her head should turn red so she understands what you mean.

Women try to cope with the hostility of their environment by internalizing male values and capitalizing on their role as mothers. It is only as mothers that they are able to command some rights and respect when they grow old.

Kemalist reforms did not reach all population groups. Islam continues to be the main frame of reference among the peasantry, as it is in small towns, cities and in the slums of metropolitan areas (Mardin, 1983; Karpat, 1976). Among the masses, religion has always been internalized as a set of 'do's and don't's' that overlap with societal conventions. This is confirmed by recent social research: most Turks interpret religiosity as being part of a community, rather than a system of personal ethics. Practices that are not prescribed in the formal religion often are adapted into this community religion. For instance, the Islamic mandates for women's right of inheritance and the bride-price can easily be overlooked in communities where there is a tradition of appropriating women's property in families which consider themselves good Muslims. Religiosity thus feeds on existing community values and strengthens them. The Islamic conservatism about gender roles has and still serves to fortify oppressive, misogynous traditions. This is quite visible in the villages.

The small town and city women

As one moves from villages to larger, semi-urban settlements such as provincial towns and smaller cities, women are increasingly withdrawn from production outside their homes: gender segregation becomes more visible. The lifestyle of women in these areas is, in many ways, more restricted than of peasant women who have a higher degree of mobility as they work outside their homes.

A foreigner entering a small Anatolian town or a provincial city might get a sense of having entered an exclusively male world: there would be very few women in sight during the day and after sunset all women would disappear from the streets. The activities of women in smaller urban settlements are confined to their homes. The change in the degree of mobility among women can even be observed in their clothing: the comfortably large, baggy trousers of a peasant woman (*shalvar*) give way to restrictive thick stockings and skirts; instead of a light, colourful blouse and vest, town women often wear heavy black coats when they go out of their homes.

Families living in these areas can roughly be divided into two groups. The first group is the locals, the families of medium or large landowners, merchants and artisans. They are generally conservative people, keen on matters relating to religion, honour and reputation. The other group is the non-local families of public servants, military and government officials. The locals can afford to let their wives stay at home. They may allow their daughters to finish primary school or even pursue higher education to learn sewing at a technical school for girls or become school teachers. This would be allowed so the girl can achieve a desirable marriage and be a better housewife. Increasing a girl's options in the labour market is usually not an objective as it is believed a woman should work only inside her home: honourable families do not raise daughters to become slaves to wage-labour.

Studies, although scarce, indicate that around 3–6% of women in small towns and cities work for income. Some of these are professionals, such as doctors and teachers, and some women take clerical jobs. Women from less advantaged families work as housemaids and laundresses. Most women, however, have home-based jobs such as knitting, sewing and weaving. Except for the professionals, these women work to contribute to the family income. They are normally ready to leave their jobs whenever the family finances improve.

Observation of relations among women in their segregated world sometimes makes a favourable impression on Westerners who perceive that this gives women a sense of psychological independence from men.

The world of most women is the private world of the house and courtyard, with a complex social structure of its own. Women organize, participate and conduct a wide range of work activities, sociability and ceremonies at a distance from the world of men. To it they bring their own leaders, skilled specialists and loyal followers. The separate structure allows freedom of action for women, away from men.

The husband is very often chosen for a woman by her family. Since she does not take full responsibility for the choice, she feels less than full responsibility for the outcome. Women do not expect men to be a major source of companionship, comfort or help in the daily work of the house. They appreciate 'worthwhile' men, but are actually slightly contemptuous of all men and feel that they are a burden to be borne.

My conclusion, which may seem paradoxical, is that women of this secluded world are in many respects more independent than the 'emancipated' women I know in Europe and America. . . . When these women enter public life they act as 'professionals', interacting with the part of their person which is trained and skilled. They do not act as total personalities and certainly not as 'females'. It is this ability to focus on their skills, to have habits and behaviour which do not necessitate orientation to men as males, which makes me find them different from women I know in the United States. American women have such a drive to relate themselves to males that whatever they do, whether personal or professional, is very often done for some man, in some way. Turkish women who work in the public sphere bring with them from the separated world of women a sense of independence of men which makes them more able to concentrate on the tasks at hand. (Fallers and Fallers, 1976)

Gender segregation probably does decrease psychological and emotional interdependence. Generally, segregated women do not worry about being physically attractive or whether they will be able to find a spouse and fulfil their biological roles. Nearly every chaste woman will become a wife and the mother of a family, sooner or later. One need not fear a life of loneliness. Neither do women worry about the approval of men when they are engaged in some asexual task, such as work, that does not threaten their chastity. Compared to some other countries (including Indonesia, South Korea, the Philippines, Singapore, Taiwan, Thailand and the USA), the level of joint decision-making, role sharing and communication between spouses is found to be lowest in Turkish families (Kagitcibasi, 1981). The inner worlds of men and women are separate.

Women are often, among themselves, scornful of men and think of them as overgrown, irrational and conceited children. Neither gender seems to feel a great emotional need for the other. However, this is in an environment where all decision-making is the privilege of men, and the limits of whatever psychological or physical independence a woman can exercise are often defined by men. The practical supports women give each other, the scorn they feel about men and the hesitant, gentle unity they exhibit in response to outbursts of unreasonable male demands are a necessary survival mechanism.

Attitudes in the families of non-local officers and public servants in these small settlements are somewhat more liberal, bearing elements of big city relationships. The educational status of the women is generally higher, some women are employed in clerical and professional jobs, and they send their daughters to high school and university. Because non-locals are scrutinized by the locals, the latter exert some control over patterns of non-local behaviour. Non-local women, for instance, may wear Western-style clothing and not cover their hair, but they do these things discreetly. That they leave their homes for shopping is overlooked but even a non-local woman may not enter a restaurant, or sit in a coffee shop unchaperoned. Neither local nor non-local girls are permitted to flirt with boys. Socializing in mixed groups is condoned among non-locals. When socializing with the locals, gender segregation is observed.

Thus the lifestyle of local women in towns and small cities is more restrictive than that of both peasant and big-city women. For a peasant woman, who is used to being out of doors interacting with nature, confinement at home and in a courtyard is a kind of imprisonment. Similarly, a big city woman reacts negatively to the extensive control and gender segregation in the smaller communities. Neither of them questions the pattern of male dominance: the housewife and mother ideal is accepted. If these women ever desire anything to add to their happiness, it is usually no more than a little more freedom of physical movement.

The squatter settlement women

Between 13% and 65% of the large urban population in Turkey live in *gecekondu* or squatter areas. *Gecekondu* means something that appears overnight. It refers to houses clandestinely built during one night on state property. People work all night and when morning comes, a structure with four walls and a roof has been erected and a family have moved in. Police may not tear down this dwelling without a court order. As it can take several years to get such an order, the residents continue to live there. Other gecekondus are successively built during this time, so that when a court order finally is issued, a whole district may already have emerged. It is difficult for government forces to demolish these houses without evoking public indignation. Usually a compromise is reached, with the government granting the land to the squatters.

The gecekondu area is the solution rural immigrants (and the government) have found to the housing shortage in big Turkish cities. They are slum-dwelling areas with low standards which have become, as in other less-developed countries, a permanent feature of urban life in Turkey. Compared to the slums of other less-developed countries, the Turkish gecekondus have a pleasant appearance – although constructed with sub-standard materials, the houses are neatly white-washed, with red tile roofs and small gardens. In some respects, the slum dwelling is a more humane abode than the impersonal, concrete high-rise apartment buildings which house the middle and upper classes of the big cities.

The squatter districts are inhabited by people from the rural areas. These people exist on the margins of urban life – in terms of productive activities as well as values and lifestyles (Senyapili, 1978). Most people work in the service sector, but a large proportion lack social insurance cover and stable working conditions. They work as janitors, peddlers, street vendors, servants and cleaners. A smaller percentage work in industry. Incomes are low.

People attempt to re-establish family and regional connections in the gecekondu as often as possible. A male newcomer typically first moves as a guest into the home of his closest relative or a friend from the same village. After securing an income, he sends for his family and they erect their own house in the same neighbourhood. Thus a neighbourhood would often contain a number of relatives or village friends, just as in the countryside. Although each family has its own abode, relations within a neighbourhood are so intense they resemble traditional extended family relations.

The average gecekondu family is nuclear. The average age at marriage is between 18 and 20, somewhat higher than in the village. An arranged marriage is the norm but opportunities for self-initiative are greater. Payment of bride-price is less common and families have fewer children. Families are stable, divorce and criminality rates are low (Senyapili, 1978).

The status of women is defined largely by traditional values: chastity, obedience and religion are important. A woman staying in her home and a breadwinning male are considered the ideal family. Standards upheld in the village are not always adhered to because of high aspirations for upward mobility and the adoption of consumption patterns of the urbanites.

Daughters are sent to school. Families make an effort to let their children study as much and as long as possible. Although only a very small minority of young people can achieve high school or university level, many daughters receive five to eight years of schooling, much more than that of their parents.

After school years, girls withdraw to their home and wait for a suitable spouse to become known. They spend that period helping their mothers with housework, reading illustrated magazine love stories, watching soap operas and day-dreaming about attaining the lifestyle and consumption level of an urban housewife. For lower-class women, becoming a good consumer usually does not go any further than dreaming about a new television set or a more effective detergent. Studies show that men spend more money and consume more than women do in Turkey. Throughout the rural–urban nexus, it is men who patronize commercial entertainment and recreational facilities. It is also men who make optimal use of political and other organizations. Men from the lower classes even dress and eat better than their women (Kandiyoti, 1977; Baysal, 1979). Squatter district women do not participate in urban life or take advantage of its cultural, recreational or political services. Neither do they purchase anything more luxurious than an occasional statuette, for example, to decorate their homes. They confine themselves to the female networks in their immediate neighbourhoods and are informed about the larger world mostly through their husbands and the mass media. In this sense, as well as others, there are many similarities between the lives of gecekondu women and their immigrant sisters in Europe.

A minority of unmarried women are employed as industrial workers or in the service sector as manicurists, office clerks and cashiers. They normally leave their jobs after marriage. Approximately 3–5% of gecekondu women are employed outside their homes. The low level of employment is partly due to the structure of the economy (the employment level of men is also low – about 50%), as well as to the fact that the first-generation female gecekondu population is unqualified for many of the few urban jobs available. Insufficient opportunity also inhibits the prospects for members of the younger generation to get a suitable job other than as a housemaid or unskilled industrial worker.

Women who work outside the home after marriage do so because of pressing economic reasons. Employment of this category of women actually has more negative than positive effects. An employed woman is often away from her home all day. If she has small children, and no trustworthy neighbours or relatives to care for them, they are left unattended: some women tie small children to their beds or lock them in a room when going to work. In addition, she has to do all the housework. Employment does not result in personal gain for a woman as her earnings are given to the 'head of family' (husband, father, brother) who decides how it should be spent. While her income contributes to the welfare of others, the low-class woman working outside her home loses the limited amount of independent decision-making power that a housewife enjoys, at least when she does the daily shopping (Kuyas, 1982). Thus, employment is considered undesirable by many low-class women who often prefer to be, as they express it, 'ladies of their home'. Whether employed or not, low-class women perceive themselves as being under total male control and feel that men make all the important decisions (Citci, 1986). They also think this is how it should be: men should be dominant (Citci, 1986; Kuyas, 1982).

The urban middle- and upper-class women

Urban middle- and upper-class women have taken optimum advantage of the legal reforms. The age at marriage among offspring in urban families is higher because both men and women are expected to complete as much schooling as possible. Urban families encourage the education of their daughters up to at least high school level or further because they have the money to compensate for the lost labour contribution. Higher education among these groups is considered a necessity. As in more highly industrialized countries, it is no longer possible to support a family with one income in urban Turkey. More and more women have to take up outside employment in order to maintain a desired standard of living. Education becomes a necessity for middle and upper class women to secure employment (Table 3.4).

Table 3.4. Education, labour force participation and employment among urban women aged more than 12 years, 1985

Education (years)	Total (1000s)	% in labour force	% employed
0	2069	6	4
1–4		6	4
5	3888	10	6
6–11	1984	28	19
>12		75	62
Total	8889	15	10

Source: Turkish State Board of Statistics, 1988

It is an anomaly in a country where about half of all women have no or woefully inadequate schooling and where only about 10% of women in urban areas are employed, that a significant portion of women win positions in universities under highly competitive conditions. Many pursue training for professions in the natural sciences, law, engineering and medicine. In 1984, women represented 41%, 24%, 37% and 20%, respectively of the students studying these curricula (Citci, 1986). The anomaly is also reflected in the working situations of women as a whole, with about 85% of the least educated working as unpaid family labourers in agriculture, and 75% of the most educated employed in the professions. The male:female ratio of people employed in top professional and administrative positions is 3:2 (Table 3.1). The proportion of women in prestigious, previously all-male professions in Turkey in the 1960s was higher than that, for instance, in the United States

(Table 3.5). This reflects the class related nature of higher education in Turkey, common in many developing countries. Whereas women in many industrialized countries are educated and work mostly at intermediary levels, only women at the two extremes of the educational spectrum in developing countries participate in production. Women who can make a difference, that is those with intermediary levels of education, in developing countries marry and become housekeepers (Safilios-Rothschild, 1971).

Table 3.5. Percentage of women lawyers and physicians in Turkey and the United States

	Turkey	*USA*
Physicians	14	10
Lawyers	19	5

Source: Erkut, 1986

Women who enter university in Turkey typically have middle and upper-middle class backgrounds (to a greater extent than men). They tend to be less traditional, placing less importance on marriage and religion than men (Culpan and Marzotti, 1982). This group of women, when they enter the labour force, show a high degree of efficiency and professionalism. Professional Turkish women are not hindered by their gender roles and the achievement anxiety phenomenon which is said to affect women in Western societies (Horner, 1972; Kandiyoti, 1979).

Career dedication is common among women in Muslim countries. It is explained by the highly structured nature of gender roles, marriage patterns and sexual segregation. Women at every level of society are brought up to believe that their future roles as mothers and wives will be primary and that their biological needs will be satisfied within marriage, regardless of the other public roles they may be required to play. The institution of arranged marriage ensures the fulfilment of every chaste woman. Public manifestations of sexual affection, and other suggestive behaviour, are considered highly inappropriate at all levels. The conditioning of women in this respect is particularly strong. Even though urban women no longer wear veils to avoid male attention, they armour themselves with an asexual attitude when they leave their homes although this may not be apparent in their physical appearance. They normally wear make-up and prefer skirts and high heels when going to work, rather than trousers or jeans. This conveys to others that they have not abandoned their womanhood just because they have entered the public sphere. In spite of her attractive appearance, a woman would feel scandalized if a man showed interest in her.

In public, a woman does not compete with other women for male attention, neither is she anxious to gain male approval. Not only would this type of behaviour endanger her reputation, but she does not feel a need for it because she is conditioned to relate sexuality to her home and private life, and asexual career considerations to her public life. This quality of asexuality and the ability to concentrate on the tasks at hand, without orienting herself to men as males, has been commented upon by several authors as a type of psychological independence, somewhat different from that of Western women (Olson, 1985; Fallers and Fallers, 1976).

Men welcome the creation of an asexual atmosphere to reduce sexual tension and distance themselves, when they interact with women in work situations. Typically, at all levels of society, unrelated men address women either formally, as Miss, Lady, Doctor, or by terms implying they consider them as close relatives in whom they would not have a sexual interest, such as sister, daughter or *yenge* (meaning a brother's wife). Likewise, women respond to men with sexually neutral titles conveying respect: mister, teacher, sir, brother. Once asexual interaction is created with appropriate behaviour, a relationship with someone of the opposite sex often becomes more relaxed and friendly. Turkish men are very polite towards women with whom they know they will not have sex. In the absence of sexual tension, men are real gentlemen and devoted comrades to women. Some men and women develop several good, loyal friendships with members of the opposite sex where only spiritual and intellectual exchange occurs. Respective family members, once assured that no sexuality is involved, generally are not suspicious of such friendships with the opposite sex. In Turkish society, friendships are considered almost as sacred as family ties: romance comes and goes but family and friends stay.

Professional women are a minority, however, and the mother and wife roles are still primary. When a competitive career woman returns to her home, she assumes the role of a self-sacrificing mother and subservient housewife. The successful contemporary woman in Turkish society is one who balances her family with a career, with emphasis on her family. A survey of female public employees revealed that more than half of the respondents believe women should work only if necessary; 85% feel they need more information on being better housewives and mothers. Even though they are aware of gender inequality, both at home and in their offices, they do not seem motivated to struggle for change. Rather than changing the status of women in society, women want better child-care facilities and more modern household machines so they can improve their performance as housewives (Citci, 1986). Even women who have taken the greatest advantage of Kemalist reforms, and who do not hesitate to compete with men on a professional level, are not ready to sacrifice their mother–wife roles.

Educated and employed women are an asset for male society. They add to their husband's or father's income, comfort and prestige, without placing any demands on them.

In a nutshell the process works as follows: A select group of women are able to pursue educational and career goals without opposition from men because they do not pose a threat either to men's privileged status or to their traditional role. Husbands and fathers of career women are able to maintain their status as head of households while continuing not to share in the daily tasks of running the house. The daily chores of keeping a house and caring for children are performed by other women with minimal education who can be hired at relatively low wages to work as domestics, cooks, laundresses and governesses. If men can enjoy the enhanced family prestige and income that a career woman can bring without having to take much more responsibility at home, why should they object to educating their daughters and allowing their wives to pursue careers outside the home? (Erkut, 1982)

Women share the labour burden among themselves. In addition to tapping the pool of inexpensive female household labour, women with outside employment also seek the assistance of their mothers, mothers-in-law and older children. No pressure is put on men to help out. When they do, for instance by grocery shopping or setting the table for a meal, it is acknowledged with gratitude.

Most Turkish women are easy to please. Middle-class women feel satisfied if they occasionally make joint decisions with their husbands. Usually the decisions concern matters of relative unimportance. The vital life matters, for which a woman's husband assumed responsibility at the time of their marriage, are not decided democratically. Men have the last word on matters concerning a woman's physical mobility, employment, political preferences, and matters of birth control and sexuality. Women cannot intervene in the decisions of their husbands in these areas. On the other hand, women exercise control in decisions on children, family activities, the family budget and small purchases. Turkish women feel satisfied with this (Kuyas, 1982).

Because outside employment is something women generally do as an extension of their mother–wife roles, neither their jobs, nor the income generated, is liberating for them. This is particularly true of the intermediate and less-educated groups of urban women. A sense of liberation is felt only in the top income and education brackets, where women's incomes are not claimed for family needs. Even at that level, the liberation effect is closely related to the father's or husband's income and educational status. Male authority decreases in Turkish families where the couple has high levels of income and education. This is contrary to patterns in industrialized countries where women's work and income in the lower brackets of society leads to more egalitarian relations, while male authority in families increases parallel to male education and income (Öncu, 1979). Women's liberation in Turkey, even in the upper classes, is not a right that is acquired, but is given to them by men.

In the urban middle and upper classes, overt manifestations of gender segregation as well as religious dogmatism are fewer. Men and women socialize and work together. But male–female relationships are carefully kept at a distanced level. Norms of honourable behaviour which exclude extramarital sexual relations, emphasizing virginity and chastity, are still highly operative. After adolescence, girls are expected to show modesty and avoid close contact with the opposite sex. Even though boys and girls go to coeducational schools and some liberal families let their daughters date and mix with unrelated boys to some extent, such socializing usually takes place in public places – coffee shops, restaurants, movies or discotheques – always in groups. If a romance or an intimate relationship develops, it is kept secret and expected to result in marriage. The double standard regarding sexual behaviour is very strong: girls who experience intimacy with boys acquire a bad reputation and are not considered desirable marriage partners but boys are expected to take advantage of all 'easy' girls. Male–female interactions are tense and distrustful. Modern big-city women have exposed hair and faces, they wear revealing clothing and join the company of men. Under these circumstances, continuing suspicions about the abuse of female sexuality and norms of honour require that women protect themselves against male attention by developing powerful internal controls and by learning the elements of asexual behaviour.

In cities arranged marriages continue to be the primary method of obtaining a spouse, but the woman's opinion of the proposed husband is usually taken into account. In 13% of marriages women make the selection and persuade their families to consent (Timur, 1979). The majority of the 13% come from the urban middle and upper classes. Approval of the families is still considered to be of utmost importance. A couple who decide otherwise may be forced to elope and risk losing financial and other support from their families.

Conclusions

Social studies, including two nationwide surveys (Kagitcibasi, 1981; Timur, 1979) and general public opinion confirm that male prerogatives and authority are unquestioned in every section of Turkish society. Kemalist reforms have been instrumental in granting women basic human rights, and greater educational and employment opportunities. But these reforms have not, to any great extent, changed the basic beliefs and attitudes inspired by Islamic ideology and the honour ethic.

In traditional settings, where Islam is practised as a community religion, religiosity and the concept of honour overlap, reinforcing each other. Gender segregation, a fundamental of Islamic dogma, is most visible in these settings. With increased affluence in urban environments, overt gender segregation is abandoned and the honour ethic becomes the determinant. Gender differentiation is typified by the double standards and mutual distrust between men and women, compelling women to internalize male controls and develop asexual behaviour patterns. Women are, at all levels, captives of values which regard their potentially uncontrolled sexuality as dangerous and disruptive.

Women lack autonomy in decision-making in the most vital areas of their existence. At all levels of society, decisions regarding women's social and biological behaviour are made by the men in their families. Relationships with, and responsibilities to, the larger family, and economic and kinship ties are more important than companionship between genders. Lack of communication is sustained by the highly structured nature of gender roles, the satisfaction each gender receives from his or her own-sex friendships and support networks, and the high value placed on a stable, unbroken family.

The ideal of a family with a full-time housewife leads to an under-estimation of women's productive activities. The labour force participation of rural women is not acknowledged, not even by themselves. The outside employment of women in urban areas is frequently regarded as necessary to the welfare of their families. Even the egalitarian Kemalist civil code does not properly regard women's rights, as human beings, to outside employment; but relates it to their duty as homemakers. Whatever work women do, and the income generated thereby, is thus regarded as an extension of their basic roles as wife and mother. Neither work nor income has a liberating effect on women when measured in terms of independent decision-making.

A slight 'liberation' effect occurs only at the top levels of society where the incomes of men are sufficient to free women's incomes from essential family expenditures and where men have reached a sufficient level of intellectual sophistication to regard women as human beings deserving equal opportunities. Even at this level, women's rights to autonomy remain something that is given to them by men.

4. Immigration

One of the most important features of economic growth in Europe following World War II and prior to the energy crisis of 1973 has been its dependence on the use of immigrant labour recruited mainly from the less industrialized countries of Europe, North Africa and the Asian subcontinent. This labour force consisted primarily of workers who migrated with official permits issued through the recruiting agencies established in the countries of origin as a result of bilateral agreements. The number of immigrants increased as workers were joined by their families. Other workers arranged for jobs through informal channels. Political refugees added to the bulk of foreign workers in Europe. The net result was that millions of people from less industrialized countries settled in Western Europe over the relatively short period of two decades. Receiving countries in Europe were West Germany, the Netherlands, Belgium, the United Kingdom, France, Austria, Switzerland, Norway and Sweden.

The industrialized countries were motivated to import foreign labour for demographic reasons, such as changing age structure and slow population growth; social reasons such as the high level of education and tendency towards early retirement; and economic reasons, such as rapid growth and full employment rates. The latter were the most important: there was a labour shortage in the less desirable jobs. For instance when West Germany first began importing workers in 1961, there were half a million job vacancies sought by 180,000 people (Sen, 1990). By contrast, governments in less developed countries were struggling with high unemployment rates and low standards of living. These countries welcomed the idea of exporting their surplus workers: it would help alleviate their unemployment problems and provide them with much needed foreign exchange.

Initially, most receiving countries recruited labour on a temporary basis. It was expected that workers would return home when the precipitating conditions changed. In Germany, foreign labourers were referred to as guest workers. Social investments which would have improved the living standards of foreign workers and helped them to integrate with the host society were seldom carried out. This led to tensions between immigrants and the host population. In response, receiving countries tightened their immigration policies. The energy crisis of the 1970s was followed by economic stagnation and rising unemployment rates: social tensions were further sharpened and new labour recruitment was banned (Paine, 1974; Abadan-Unat, 1982; Kudat and Frey, 1975; Sen, 1990). However, emigration of relatives as well as political refugees continued.

Foreign labour generally made a positive impact on the economy of the host countries. It had a counter-inflationary effect and contributed to accelerated economic growth. Employers gained access to inexpensive and unorganized labour which was willing to take the jobs the indigenous workers found undesirable (Paine, 1974; Abadan-Unat, 1982). Home countries also profited; the remittances of workers became an important resource for shrinking budget deficits. The remittances of Turkish workers in 1975 and 1981, for example, equalled 65% and 48% respectively of the total export earnings of Turkey during those years (Maillat, 1986).

Despite the original scheme, it became clear with time that it would be difficult for immigrants to return home and foreign labour became a permanent feature of the European economy.

Turkish Immigration to Europe

> Now the eyes of four children back in Eregli bulge with hunger . . .
>> My forefathers were too mighty for today and tomorrow;
>> I fell, I flounder, a servant for foreigners now.
> Why stay behind? For a thousand green marks a month,
> Let's spread out from eagle Anatolia to the face of the earth
>>> Come on, let's sweep their streets,
> Huge brooms, towering garbage,
> Unashamed in the face of the crimson sun,
>> Hands filthy, hearts filthy.
> My forefathers were too mighty for today and tomorrow;
> I fell, I flounder, a servant for foreigners now.
>>>>>>>> F. H. Daglarca (Halman, 1985)

When labour migration began, Turkey was still an agricultural country. In 1963, 41% of the national income and over 80% of exports were agricultural products such as cotton, tobacco, dried fruit and hazelnuts. Seventy-seven percent of the labour force was engaged in agriculture. Only 10% of the population was employed in industry, contributing 17% of the national income. The deficit in the balance of payments was large and growing; inequalities in income within regions and between regions were severe (Paine, 1974).

An agreement with West Germany for recruiting workers from Turkey was negotiated in 1961. Labour agreements with other countries followed. Turkish labour quickly became popular: employers preferred Turks over workers from other countries because they were less likely to join labour unions, were not demanding, had a higher level of work discipline and were more content with the standards of housing they were offered. They were a docile work force, ready to do anything that would secure an honest income (Abadan-Unat, 1964; Sen, 1990).

Recruitment offices were established in the major cities of Turkey. Prospective workers were called in to make application and be interviewed. This was followed by a medical check-up to ensure that the worker was in good health. If found eligible, the worker waited until a vacancy arose in the host country. Normally, the employer paid for the passport and travel expenses. The migrant began work immediately after arriving in the host country. Significant numbers of workers who were in great financial need and could not afford to wait for a vacany left Turkey unofficially as tourists. They arranged for jobs with the help of friends or relatives; job vacancies were readily available when mass migration began. The emigration of workers peaked in 1967. By 1970, Turkey had become, after Yugoslavia, the second largest supplier of labour to Western Europe.

In the mid-1980s, official census figures estimated two million Turkish citizens were living in Western Europe (Table 4.1); because of naturalizations, children born of mixed marriages and other factors such as illegal migration, the actual number is probably closer to three million. At present, the greatest representation of Turkish workers is in Germany, with an estimated population of about two million, constituting 34% of the foreign population. Following a bilateral agreement with the Netherlands in 1964, some 30,000 Turks entered this country with work permits through 1970. By 1981, their numbers had increased five-fold to 148,000. Turks now constitute the greatest proportion of foreign workers in the Netherlands (27%). Workers were allowed to enter Belgium as tourists and were readily granted work and residence permits once they secured employment. In 1977, Turkish citizens in Belgium constituted about 7% of the foreign population, with some 80,000 living there. Turkish representation in other countries such as France (about 170,000), Switzerland (around 60,000), Sweden and Denmark (30,000) constitutes about 3–5% of total foreign populations (Castles *et al*, 1984). Turkish workers are poorly represented in Britain. Until 1962, Turkish Cypriots could freely enter the UK as Commonwealth citizens. There was little interest among Turks from

Table 4.1. Number of Turkish citizens in some European countries, (1982) thousands

	Turkish citizens	*All foreign citizens*
West Germany	1581	4667
Belgium	66	886
France	123	3680
Netherlands	152	538
Sweden	20	406
Switzerland	47	960

Source: Maillat, 1986

the mainland to work in Britain during the 1960s because of demand in other European countries. No bilateral labour agreement was reached between Turkey and Britain. When European countries began to ban labour migration in the 1970s, however, the UK became a desirable alternative for emigration. By this time, securing employment in the UK had become very difficult. Unknown numbers of Turks entered as tourists and worked illegally. Official figures are difficult to find but it is estimated there are about 60,000 Turks in the UK, of which about two-thirds are Cypriots. Turkish Cypriots are well-established in society, while those who come from the mainland work illegally, often under very exploitative conditions (Tasiran, personal communication).

Emigration costs money and requires contacts, even when arranged through official channels. Although financial motivation was the primary reason for migration, those who came to Europe were not the poorest. A comparison of departing workers and the economically active population in Turkey suggests that the emigrating labourers represented a positive selection (Table 4.2). A typical emigrating worker at the beginning of the migration wave was a semi-qualified, literate, married man in his early twenties from the urban areas of the prosperous Marmara/Thrace and north-central Anatolia regions. After the mid-1960s, the profile changed to that of a less literate, less qualified married man from rural Anatolia, also migrating from the relatively prosperous regions. Thus, the great majority of Turkish workers in Europe came from rural areas or had low-income, big-city backgrounds. Immigrant workers from the least developed east and south-east regions of Anatolia have always been under-represented in official immigration statistics, although some did arrive in Europe later as political refugees.

Table 4.2. Summary of selcted socio-economic characteristics of Turkish migrant workers as compared with those of the economically active population in Turkey

Characteristic	Migrant workers (%)	Economically active population in Turkey (%)
Males	84	62
From western and north-central Anatolia	62	46
Aged between 20 and 45	96	47
Married	86	90
Illiterate	8	47
Non-agricultural skilled or semi-skilled workers	67	41
Unemployed	4	10
Employed in agriculture	41	67

Source: Paine, 1974

Turkish Women in Europe

Hasan went to Germany last autumn. Hanife girl, I told myself, if only one road in a thousand leads to Germany, you're gonna find it, and you're gonna get there. They say they give workers tons of money. A worker's honour is nobody's business as long as one is strong. I'm gonna show you how strong I am, Hasan, you'll see how I'll pile up money and one day I'll sit back in a car, just like the district governor's wife. I'll sit back and order the boy to drive it to the door of the factory where you work. Hasan will be struck when he sees me, he'll say Hanife girl, you crazy girl, what are you doing here, he'll say, you should know how I missed you, he'll say, but I won't let him in my car. He'll cry his eyes out, but I won't take him to my house. He'll sleep on the porch. He'll beg me. He'll bring his mother from the village to ask me to marry him, but I'll say go away, peasant, I'm gonna marry the district governor, I'll say, and besides he's gonna be the district governor of Germany, I'll say. (Soysal, 1976)

Women were also recruited as migrant workers. In 1961, 5% of the recruited Turkish workers in West Germany were women. The recruitment of women was given higher priority in the late 1960s and increased to 16% of the total migrants in 1970. Some of these women were recruited with their husbands, while many came alone, as 'pioneers'.

The few studies on the pioneer women suggest they were generally younger, better educated and more skilled than the average economically active women in Turkey; but their numbers also included women with very little education and no previous work experience (Paine, 1974; Davis and Heyl, 1986). Some of the migrant women workers were unmarried, like Hanife above. Many married women also migrated and became the sole breadwinners of their families for some years, before they arranged jobs for their husbands. This process had profound effects on their role within the family (Kudat and Frey, 1975; Davis and Heyl, 1986).

The possibility of sending one's wife or daughter ahead, thus creating the legal ground for family reunion, created in the mentality of a great number of traditional-minded Turkish men revolutionary concepts. Women of rural background, traditionally socialized, totally unprepared mentally and to a considerable extent unwilling, were strongly urged by their fathers, husbands or other relatives to take up industrial or service jobs in foreign countries in order to secure for their male relatives the possibility of obtaining lucrative jobs with higher income possibilities in the near future. Thus a great number of Turkish women entered industrial jobs with no knowledge of city life, highly disciplined working hours and production norms. (Abadan-Unat, 1982)

Even though the odds seemed to be against them, many pioneer women succeeded in adjusting to a radically different existence: from being agricultural producers or housewives, they changed into wage earners the day they arrived in Europe. The success with which many Turkish women made these adjustments is held as proof of their psychological flexibility and strength in meeting new demands, something they are taught to do from early childhood (Kiray, 1986). Some women, however, felt the change was too rapid and suffered its consequences (Stiver Lie, 1985).

Most women were left behind in Turkey with the children. The men believed that their stay abroad would be temporary. The expectation was to return after some years of hard work and prudent saving. Although their primary motive was economic, and although they could have earned and saved more if joined by their wives in the beginning men did not wish to jeopardize their honour by bringing their wives and children into a foreign, non-Muslim environment and allowing them to work and mix with unrelated people (Merdol, 1982).

The young wives were left to live with their husbands' families. Older ones, who already had established separate households, remained with their children. At the departure of their husbands, significant changes occurred also in the roles of these women. Most suddenly found themselves in a challenging position where they were 'expected to be both man and wife' (Merdol, 1982). Those living in their own homes, in particular, became the chief decision-makers in matters relating to expenditure, distribution of responsibilities, the upbringing of the children and protection of family honour. They came into contact with public institutions such as schools, banks and government agencies. The following is an immigrant woman's description of her difficulties after her husband left.

> It was difficult because I was not used to taking care of everything. The worst was going to the grocery store. When we ran out of sugar, I would not buy more. I did not dare go to the store. Women do not go to the store – men gather there. It is almost like a coffee shop. They stand there and talk. I tried to avoid buying sugar as long as possible. I could not send the children, either. They would not have been able to carry the heavy sugar bag. I had to gather all my courage and go there myself in the end. I had never before handled money and knew nothing about prices and things. That of which I was most afraid, happened. The store was full of men. They all stared at me. Then they started making jokes: 'Look at Mustafa's wife. She has become a man!' I felt I had lost my honour. (Ertem-Kurtiz and Kuyumcu, 1985)

The men who emigrated to Europe worked as hard as possible; workers holding two or three jobs were not unusual – they reasoned that the more they worked, the sooner they would return to Turkey. In 1971, 34% of a sample of Turkish workers in West Germany intended to stay up to five years and almost 50% planned to stay for not more than ten years. Saving was more difficult than they had imagined. Establishing residence in a foreign country demanded extra expenditure and the dependants left behind in Turkey – an average of 4.6 persons – had to be supported. An average worker was not able to begin saving until two years after emigration. Then about 36% of the income could be saved and an additional 11% could be remitted to the family in Turkey (Aker, 1972). Life was difficult: sub-standard, crowded housing conditions, lack of recreation, loneliness, social marginalization and discrimination were daily realities.

In the 1970s, workers began to reconsider their plans: economic conditions in Turkey were deteriorating and to attain their goals, they had to prolong their stay and improve their saving strategies. Bringing their families over and letting their women work would significantly increase their incomes and improve the quality of their lives. Throughout the 1970s, large numbers of Turkish women and children migrated to Europe. Family reunions proceeded at different speeds according to legislation in different countries. The male:female ratio of Turkish immigrants is presently equal in most countries.

The following are some of the characteristics of Turkish immigrant women (Abadan-Unat, 1982):

Turkish immigrant women represent a relatively young population group. About three-fourths are younger than 35 years of age.

More than two-thirds of the employed Turkish women are married.

The highest fertility rate in Europe belongs to Turkish women.

The proportion of women who have not attended school at all is higher than among the male immigrants.

The occupational training of women is considerably less than that of men. Most Turkish woman immigrants are employed in jobs requiring no qualification.

As their primary motivation for migrating abroad, the majority of women indicate the desire to join their families. The second most important reason is economic.

Living in Europe

Ethnic and religious composition

Immigrants from Turkey are an ethnically heterogeneous group that includes Turks, Kurds, Armenians and Assyrians (Nestorian Christians), and smaller groups of Circassians, Arabs, Greeks, Kazaks, Georgians and Tartars (Svanberg, 1985). There are also non-Anatolian Turkish immigrants in Europe, such as the Turkish Cypriots, the Bulgarian, Macedonian, Bosnian, Crimean, Azeri and Afghan Turks. Of the three largest non-Turkish ethnic groups who originate primarily in eastern Anatolia, the Kurds are Muslims, and Assyrians and Armenians belong to the Orthodox Christian church. Each of these groups speaks a different language. The discussion in this book is limited to Anatolian Turks who speak the Anatolian Oghuz dialect of Turkish as their mother tongue and are either Sunni or Alevi Muslims.

Anatolian Turkish immigrants in Europe originate primarily from the Marmara/Thrace and central Anatolia regions. As mentioned, most have low-income urban or rural backgrounds, having migrated for economic reasons or to join family members (Paine, 1974; Abadan-Unat, 1982). A minority of Turks from large cities came to pursue studies or as political refugees. Turkish refugees seeking asylum in Europe reached peak numbers during the period 1972–83, as a result of the two military takeovers and the politically turbulent period in between. People with Kurdish ethnicity continue to seek asylum in European countries because of the assimilationist policies of successive Turkish governments.

Migrant Turkish workers established secular, shared-interest groups around cultural, political or regional affiliations. Many of these organizations are represented in the unions for Turkish Associations in the host countries.' Religious organizations are of secondary importance. Some Sunni Turks attend religious associations which are open to all Muslims regardless of nationality. A minority of the more orthodox Turks gather in religious associations which defend fundamentalism. The latter type of organization is most common in Germany (Sen, 1990), but may be gaining ground in other European countries. Generally religious associations serve as places for prayer, for meetings between Muslims and offer Koran classes for children. Alevi Turks are not organized along religious lines.

Education and occupations

Data on the educational status of Turkish immigrants is difficult to find and even more difficult to evaluate as more and more Turks obtain part of their schooling outside the home country. If five years of schooling, which is compulsory in Turkey, is taken as a demarcation point, it is found that 50% of the women and 32% of the men are either illiterate or have received less than five years of education in the home country (Table 3.2). When the first wave of migration began, the educational level of Turkish immigrants was significantly higher than national averages (Paine, 1974; Abadan-Unat, 1982), probably as a function of the fact that the departing workers were primarily from urban centres. With increased recruitment from rural areas and family reunions, the educational background of migrants reflected the national average. Table 4.3 outlines the educational status of Turkish immigrants according to a representative survey carried out in Sweden in 1975 (Alpay, 1985). Table 3.2 suggests that Turkish immigrant men, particularly those with urban backgrounds, had higher levels of education than the national average. The opposite was true for women. The difference between men and women was

Table 4.3. Educational status of Turkish immigrants in Stockholm (percentage)

Years of	Men		Women	
Education	Rural	Urban	Rural	Urban
<4	24	12	79	30
5–10	70	46	21	56
>10	6	42	–	15

Source: Alpay, 1980

greatest at the lowest educational levels. This observation is of limited value in terms of judging the educational levels of the Turkish immigrant populations in general, because the second and third generation Turks no longer receive home-country schooling. It can only tentatively be assumed that the educational level tends to be low for women and that a given number of first generation women may be expected to be illiterate, depending on their region of origin. The large literacy differential between first generation Turkish immigrant men and women decreases with the second generation, but the proportion of girls who do not complete nine years of schooling (which is the compulsory length in most European countries) may still be expected to be about twice as high as it is for boys (Similä, 1987; Jeppesen, 1989).

Before coming to Europe, most men were self-employed as farmers, small businessmen or craftsmen. A majority of women were housewives; very few had professional jobs. The great majority of women from rural areas were engaged in agriculture (Paine, 1974; Alpay, 1985; Merdol, 1982). Most migrant Turks obtain manual jobs which require minimal qualifications (Paine, 1974; Abadan-Unat, 1982; Castles *et al*, 1984). The most common jobs are factory and construction work and cleaning, according to the country of emigration. Turkish women in Sweden and Denmark hold predominantly cleaning and dishwashing jobs. In Norway and the Netherlands they also work in the clothing and food packaging industries. They work as domestic servants and in the textile, chemical, clothing, food packaging and electronics industries of Germany. They work as seamstresses and cleaners in France. In the UK, they are concentrated in the clothing and catering industries, often working in poor conditions (Tasiran, 1989). The following description is from England.

A sweatshop is the best description for the Turkish woman's workplace. Her workday begins at 8 a.m. and often does not end until 7:30–8:30 p.m. The derelict, rundown building is cold in the winter and hot in the summer. No lunch facilities are provided so she has to eat lunch by the machine. Two toilets service the entire factory. . . . From Christmas until May she is often made redundant. That's the time the bosses deliberately fiddle the books. The change of the tax year is approaching – books show lower wages so the owner avoids redundancy payments when he lays off staff. Then they may declare bankruptcy, open under a new name, and carry on. Because of this she works longer hours during the rest of the year. . . . If she complains the employer tells her to go – but where? Too weary in the evenings to take English or educational courses, she has no prospects for the future. She resists becoming a union member for fear of being labelled traitor to the Turkish community. (Stiver Lie, 1985)

Working conditions are somewhat better in countries with better employment regulations. However, the nature of the jobs Turkish women hold are significantly more monotonous, dirtier and physically more demanding than the jobs of other foreign groups or of the indigeneous populations in all countries (Stiver Lie, 1985, Castles *et al*, 1984).

A second category, consisting mostly of the children of immigrants, is semi-qualified manual workers such as cooks, cashiers or industrial workers. Only about one-fifth of Turkish migrants work in non-manual, qualified jobs such as teaching, translating or in professional occupations. The majority of the latter group have urban backgrounds in Turkey or are second generation immigrants.

Employment rates at the beginning of the 1980s were very high. In Sweden, 84% of Turkish men and about 60% of women were employed (Jonung, 1982). It was common for men to have two or three jobs: a man would work on an assembly line during the day, wash dishes in the evening, and have a part-time job as a janitor at weekends (Alpay, 1980). Women might work two cleaning shifts and do piece-work as seamstresses over weekends. In some countries, Turkish women (together with Yugoslavs) constituted the most highly employed nationality in the female labour force (Stiver Lie, 1985). Following reunions, other family members were expected to begin work as soon as possible. Initial concern about allowing women to work outside their homes was overcome, largely because of eagerness to maximize income, but also because jobs such as cleaning or taking sewing orders at home do not require extensive contact with others. Women were often able to work in all-Turkish, all-female groups, without meeting men (Merdol, 1982).

Employment rates among Turks have been declining. In Sweden in 1985, rates had fallen to 51% and 44%, respectively, for men and women (State Board of Statistics, 1985). In 1988, two-thirds of Turks in Germany were receiving unemployment or welfare compensation (Sen, 1990). Turkish women were the worst affected, despite their high motivation to work (Stiver Lie, 1985; Jeppesen, 1989; Petek-Salom and Hüküm, 1986).

One of the key reasons for the current low employment rate of Turkish migrants is the often marginal nature of their occupations: unqualified workers lose their jobs faster than those who are qualified. Other factors are that immigrants enter the labour force later than indigenous workers ('last in, first out'); concentrate in production areas that decline faster than others during times of recession (such as the textile, construction and electronics industries); and suffer informal discrimination against immigrants in hiring, promoting and firing (Castles *et al*, 1984).

A study carried out in Germany in 1980 shows that Turks are a particularly disadvantaged group. It was found that 27% of men and 40% of women in all foreign groups held unqualified jobs, but that after some time in employment, an average of 43% of foreigners were promoted to a position where they could perform more qualified tasks. Among Turks, 35% of men and 55% of women had unqualified jobs and only 35% were promoted. The authors conclude that Turkish workers have the lowest socio-economic status in the German labour market and that their options for changing this situation are very limited, a finding which can only be explained by the fact that they constitute the group most discriminated against in Germany. The status of Turkish workers in Europe is found comparable to that of the black population in the UK (Castles *et al*, 1984).

The socially isolated nature of the working environment limits options for interaction with the host society, which contributes to difficulties in learning the new language. Turkish is very different from most European languages (with the exception of Hungarian and Finnish). It is difficult enough for young, literate people with efficient study habits to learn European languages; it becomes even more so when one has little general education, and it is almost impossible if one does not have the opportunity to practise the new language in everyday situations, such as at work. Their educational background and the nature of the jobs they hold in Europe make it difficult for Turks to learn the language of their host countries which would help them acquire new skills to improve their occupational status – a vicious circle which leads to further marginalization. There is, however, a new eagerness to change this pattern ('Raise your voice', 1985).

Age, sex and family composition

Emigration can often lead to family fragmentation. Considering the importance Turks place on family unity, the splintering of families as fathers, sons, mothers and daughters left in the 1960s to work in Europe had traumatic effects. Despite family reunions in the 1970s, most immigrants are still separated from members of their families (Abadan-Unat, 1982).

The male:female ratio of Turkish citizens in Europe has now stabilized with a slight surplus of men. Turks marry at a younger age than any other nationality in Europe (Leiniö, 1988; Merdol, 1982; Similä, 1987; Jeppesen, 1989). Nearly 65% of women marry before 20 years of age. The majority of marriages are arranged and about half involve payment of a bride-price. About a third of all marriages are to a relative, usually a first or second cousin (Similä, 1987; Merdol, 1982; Jeppesen, 1989).

Divorce rates among Turkish male immigrants are similar to those of other immigrant men. The highest divorce rates occur when spouses are not living in the same country or among marriages between people of different nationalities. Divorce rates are lowest among Turkish women. During the period 1971–84, nine out of a thousand marriages in Sweden were dissolved by Turkish women. Comparable figures for Yugoslav and Finnish immigrant women were twenty-one and nineteen per thousand, respectively (Leiniö, 1988). These figures may be misleading as they do not include divorces decreed in the courts of the home country but nonetheless indicate a desire for stable marriages among women, particularly Turkish women. It is normal for all young or unmarried children in a family to live together in a single household (Jeppesen, 1989). Family size differs according to background in Turkey. In West Germany in 1975, a Turkish woman had 4.3 children on average (as compared to 1.3 children for German women). This rate decreased to 3.4 by 1981, and confirms the finding that the fertility rate of Turkish immigrant women is falling (Maillat, 1986; School, 1984; Merdol, 1982).

While a nuclear family, consisting of parents and their unmarried children, is the rule, extended families and families sharing a common domicile also exist among people with rural backgrounds. In the case of extended families, the marrying child brings his or her spouse to the parental home where they live for a few years, similar to the practice in Turkey. In Turkey, however, it is normal for a woman to join her husband's family. Among immigrants, it is quite common to find men joining the family of their brides. There are also 'share' families where two relatives (siblings or cousins), together with their respective spouses and children, share the same household (Merdol, 1982; Nauck, 1989). These family formations are partially an extension of Turkish traditions, but are also precipitated by the nature of chain-migration.

In extended families, the young couple moves to a separate home after a few years, when they have paid off the loans incurred by the bride-price (if any), the wedding and the travel expenses of the newly arrived spouse. The separate nuclear households are typically established in close vicinity to one another. Couples sometimes live in the same block or apartment building as their parents, married siblings, nieces and nephews. Although families are structurally nuclear, they function as extended families. Mutual help and support networks are strong. Everyone knows what is going on in the other households and feels a responsibility for all other family members. The close ties among households provide security and act as a buffer against the alienation and isolation which those living in a foreign environment face.

Lifestyles in Europe

Social class differences in Turkish society are highly obvious. Clothing, language and gestures give clues. The cultural distance between Turks with big city backgrounds and higher levels of education and those with rural or low educational backgrounds is about as great as the differences between Western European and Turkish society in general. Because the majority of immigrant Turks have rural or low income urban backgrounds where cultural norms are more strongly defined by traditions, the following characteristics generally concern this category. The accounts are generalizations. Individual cases will vary.

Social networks
Immigrant Turks are socially segregated from the larger society. Social contacts are almost exclusively with family, kin and countrymen. If friendships outside the Turkish community are established, these are usually with other immigrants, most often with Greeks as cultural affinities between the two countries transcend political hostilities.

Contact with members of the host population is extremely limited; there is mutual feeling of a large cultural distance (Bergman and Svendin, 1982; Bendix, 1985; Alpay, 1980; Toelken, 1985). Unlike Mediterranean peoples, many Europeans prefer solitary leisure time pursuits to socializing. The language barrier also inhibits social contact, but this is probably of secondary importance: when socializing with other immigrant groups, Turks do not feel the lack of a common language to be a hindrance.

Adaptation and attitudes

Adapting to a new society not only depends on the degree of cultural similarity but also on an individual's expectations for the future. Those who plan to stay in a new country for a long time, or permanently, are more likely to strive for integration. Permanent residence in Europe was not an objective for the early immigrants. Survey findings from the 1970s and early 1980s indicate that only about 20% of Turks had decided to stay, while another 20% were undecided and 60% planned to return to the home country at some time in the future. Only a few were precise about the planned time of their return. The desire to return is stronger among immigrants from rural areas and among those working in unskilled or semi-skilled manual jobs (Alpay, 1980; Merdol, 1982).

As the cost of living in Turkey soars, the amount of money that must be saved and invested increases each year. The cultural distance between immigrants and their home country also grows as they become more acquainted with Europe, as their children grow and as society in Turkey changes. Many Turks are beginning to admit that they probably will not be able to return home. This is observable in new career orientations and consumption patterns: Turks have recently begun setting up small businesses and investing in consumer durables and better housing in their new countries. Such behaviour was unusual about a decade ago, when most Turks still believed they would be returning home (Sen, 1990).

When evaluating the immigration experience, Turks point out that their material standards have improved: incomes, housing, schools, sickness and old-age security systems are better than in Turkey. The majority are also satisfied with their work, particularly those who are employed in qualified or semi-qualified jobs. Even those working in unqualified jobs are satisfied with their income and the working conditions (Alpay, 1980; Similä, 1987). They are most satisfied with marriage, followed by life achievements; satisfaction with work takes third place. Turks are least satisfied with the rights and opportunities they have in Europe (Nauck, 1989). The democratic functioning of European societies, freedom of assembly and expression, the effectiveness of institutions, the work ethic and the welfare system are highly appreciated. Turks are, however, critical of how children are brought up, sexual freedom, family relations, leisure time activities and the quality of food in Europe.

Turks feel that emigration lessens their chances of achieving respect in society. This is a realistic appraisal: Turks are one of the groups most discriminated against in Europe (Bendix, 1985; Bergman and Svendin, 1982; Toelken, 1985; Castles *et al*, 1984). This discrimination can be vulgar and cruel as evidenced in the following Swedish joke.

> An American, a Turk and a Swede meet at the top of the Eiffel Tower. Each begins bragging about his own country. The American says: 'We have a lot of money in America,' takes out dollars from his pocket and begins throwing them down from the tower. Then the Turk says, 'We have a lot of heroin in Turkey,' takes out heroin packages from his pocket and begins throwing them around. Then the Swede says, 'We have a lot of Turks in Sweden,' and takes the Turk and throws him down.

There are many jokes about Turks in West Germany (Toelken, 1985):

Have you seen the latest German microwave?
It has room for a whole Turkish family.

A Jew and a Turk jump out of an airplane at the same time; which one hits
the ground first?
Does it make a difference?

A Turkish train with a crowd of people on board leaves Istanbul, but arrives
later in Frankfurt entirely empty. Why?
It travelled by way of Auschwitz.

Turks react by isolating themselves (Bendix, 1985). Immigrants also lose
socio-economic status: a previously independent farmer or small entrepreneur
may become a cleaner or dishwasher. Most urban professionals do not manage
to find employment commensurate with their qualifications.

Turks consider themselves as having attained certain personal goals and are
satisfied with what the emigration experience has offered them within these
limits. When compared with other immigrants in Sweden, for instance, Turks
stand out as one of the most isolated but, at the same time, the most satisfied
and optimistic group (Alpay, 1980). There is no great bitterness against
Western society. Despite their awareness of being marginalized and
discriminated against, and that they stand at the lowest level of the social
hierarchy in most of Europe, Turks feel their lifestyles and moral values are
above reproach and this gives them a sense of self-worth which transcends the
attitudes of outsiders.

This self-confidence is attributable to the strong identification with the home
country (Alpay, 1980; Merdol, 1982; Similä, 1987; Jeppesen, 1989; Aronowitz,
1988). Turks hold on to their traditional culture and identity as a defensive
reaction to their rejection by Western culture. The more homogeneous is the
dominant culture, the more Turks isolate themselves and identify with their
home culture (Kagitcibasi, 1987).

Decision-making in the family

The Turkish family is idealized: the major criticism of Western lifestyles is that
the Western family is considered very unstable. This instability is believed to be
caused by the absence of norms designating mutual duties and responsibilities
among family members. Blame is assigned to the excessive autonomy of
women which leads to neglect of their duties as wives and mothers, and to
methods of child-rearing which foster individualism, leading youngsters to feel
no responsibility or respect for others. A goal among all Turks in Europe is to
preserve the stable, close-knit traditional family structure.

Idealization of the Turkish family leads to the defence of traditional roles
played by, and responsibilities placed upon, each of the members. When
defining family relations, the hierarchies of age and gender are cited as categories

which have not changed and which should remain intact. Men maintain their roles as major decision-makers in areas of women's sexuality, family economics, relations with the public and children's schooling; women tend to the upbringing of children and housework (Similä, 1987; Merdol, 1982; Alpay, 1980).

Some important changes in decision-making are occurring. Women are now fighting for education for their daughters, for their rights to gainful employment and to choice of spouse (Petek-Salom and Hüküm, 1986; Merdol, 1982; Jeppesen, 1989). Turkish women are beginning to influence the sexual behaviour of their husbands, by showing less tolerance for their adulterous adventures (which are likely to be taken for granted in Turkey) (Kudat and Frey, 1975). Women are exercising more autonomy in economic matters (Kudat and Frey, 1975; Merdol, 1982; Kocturk-Runefors, 1988). The status of women in the family influences a variety of things, including housing standards, utilization of cultural facilities of the home and host countries and the degree of integration with the host society (Nauck, 1989). Even relations with the public are ceasing to be an exclusively male domain: women are the main mediators of contact with authorities (Mortensen, 1989). Nonetheless, the primacy of the wife and mother role, the sexual behaviour norms of women and the honour ethic remain unquestioned (Mortensen, 1990; Merdol, 1982; Davis and Heyl, 1986).

Free time
Visiting is a favourite pastime. Couples visit close friends and relatives on holidays. Informal visits and contacts with more distant acquaintances are often gender-segregated. Gender segregation is also observed in organized leisure activities such as participation in sports, political meetings and certain types of entertainment, such as eating out and going to night clubs (these are male domains). Women take courses in home-making (sewing is popular), and sometimes attend association meetings concerning women, children or the family. Women also like to go shopping during their free time.

Watching video films from the home country takes up a very significant portion of leisure time. Many of these films are sexist, depicting traditional male–female roles where women are either housewives or prostitutes and belly dancers. These films are criticized as not reflecting the realities of life in Turkey or the experiences of the immigrants (Abadan-Unat, 1982).

One organized leisure activity is relatively new to most Turkish immigrants: taking a paid vacation from work. As peasants or small business owners, most Turks are used to work cycles which shift from high to low intensity depending on the season or economic conditions. One is expected to work as long as one is physically able to; vacations are for the very young and the very old. An annual vacation, freed from regular work and other responsibilities, is a popular activity that couples share with each other. Vacations are used for visiting the home country, or friends and relatives in other parts of Europe.

Religion

It is difficult to comment on the degree to which Turks adhere to orthodox Islamic tradition. The secularization of Turkey, and the conditions under which this came about, created an aversion to religion and, later, a general lack of interest in it among a large portion of the population. Most people from urban backgrounds distance themselves from any type of religious practice.

Islam continues to influence rural residents. Due to ethnic, cultural and language differences, religious practices in Anatolia are different from those in the rest of the country. The most extreme examples are the heterodox Alevi/Bektashi beliefs. Sunni Islam in Anatolia developed as a community religion, rather than an orthodoxy. Many Anatolians practise folk religion which is described as:

> popular religiosity, national customs, Islamic rules of conduct, mysticism, folk knowledge, folklore and magic with Islamic elements – all welded into a traditional interpretation of Islam which has grown organically in Turkey. It is . . . an unsystematic and unmediated religious and cultural tradition, barely accessible to arguments and discussions. (Thomä-Venske, 1988)

The religious identity of Turks is inextricably bound to ethnic identity. Non-Turkish Muslims complain that Turks are too nationalistic (Sander, 1988), a characteristic which traditional Islamic ideology rejects, given its philosophy of the extended community (umma). Ethnic identity is paramount among Turkish immigrants, followed by identification with customs and traditions. Religious identity lags behind (Antes, 1985; Sander, 1988).

Nevertheless, religion is important. In a Stockholm study involving 16–24-year-old Turks (an age group which is not particularly concerned with religion), 50% of respondents said they pray daily; 37% want to bring up their children according to Islamic precepts, and about a third disapprove of marriages with people from other faiths (Similä, 1987). Similar findings are reported from Denmark (Jeppesen, 1989). In another study of Turks from all age groups in Berlin, 84% said they would like to raise their children according to Islamic doctrine (Thomä-Venske, 1988). Even though most Turks in Europe are not very informed about Islam, and are unable to explain the origin of their traditions, they find security in adherence to their Muslim identity. Few Turks are otherwise actively engaged in theological issues (Thomä-Venske, 1988; Antes, 1985).

In the rundown housing areas where Turks live, there is a high concentration of Westerners who are divorced, of single parent families or with drug and alcohol problems. Isolated as they are, many Turks do not have a realistic impression of the more common lifestyles in the larger host society. The general tendency is to compare themselves with the society they observe in their immediate neighbourhood and draw a (biased) conclusion that gender equality would lower their norms of social conduct.

A woman's attire and the schooling of children are the real indicators of religious attitudes. Adherence to other rules, such as daily prayer, fasting and giving alms is not conclusive evidence, as Muslims who have internalized secularism can practise these without public display of religiosity. If a woman covers her hair and wears unrevealing clothing it is highly visible testimony to the importance she accords Islamic values (Wilpert, 1988; Olson, 1985b). The style of clothing is considered the major indicator of religiosity (Petek-Salom and Hüküm, 1986). The other indicator is sending children to Koran courses where, at about the age of seven or eight, they begin to learn about the religious texts from an *imam*. Separate classes for boys and girls meet several times a week. Attendance rates fluctuate between different countries. Parents urge their children to take Koran instruction so they are protected from Western moral values. The courses are seen as a meaningful leisure time activity that will keep children under parental control and ease their re-adaptation to Turkish society when the family returns home. There is some social pressure, in Turkish neighbourhoods, to enrol children in these courses. Turkish and European pedagogues say these courses overtax children's energy, are stultifying and dogmatic, can lead to anxiety and animosity towards Western society, and discriminate against girls (Thomä-Venske, 1988). This is true only for Sunni Turks. There are groups of Alevi Turks in Europe who, as mentioned, believe Sunnis are religious fanatics and oppress women. Alevis reject outward manifestations of religiosity and carry out religious education within the hereditary family system; women are not covered, gender segregation is not practised and children do not take Koran courses (Wilpert, 1988; Naess, 1988).

5. Turkish Families meet Western Culture: A Case Study in Sweden

The Study

This chapter presents material collected during a field study involving interviews with Turkish immigrants living in the Stockholm and Uppsala counties of Sweden. The objective of the study was to describe the changes occurring in gender and family relations among Turkish immigrants. The study was carried out between September 1987 and October 1988. The interviewees, Turkish-speaking adults from Anatolia with at least one marriage or engagement experience, were reached through personal contacts. The profiles of the sample of 10 men and 49 women who participated in the study are presented in Table 5.1.

Because the main normative difference between Turkish immigrants and the host society is in the area of gender and family relations, there was a general wariness about discussing these subjects. It was thus difficult to find volunteers to participate in the study. Men were more sceptical than women and most declined to participate. Women were generally more interested, but many were reluctant to participate without first consulting their fathers or husbands. Some women subsequently declined.

The men who participated typically had urban backgrounds, were better educated, had better jobs and were more often unmarried at the time of the study than the women who participated. Seven men had been married at least once or had cohabited with a non-Turkish woman. The men in the sample represented an elite selection of Turkish male immigrants. The men were generally more reluctant than the women to discuss their personal lives. Most men preferred to give their opinions about more general problems concerning the immigrant situation. This resulted in an under-representation of the personal experiences of men in the analysis. The women, who were of rural origins and less educated, better reflect a cross-section of immigrant Turkish women. Participating women can be divided into two groups: those who felt independent enough to discuss their lives confidentially and give their opinions, and those who had problems in these areas and wished to relate them. Most of the women were married, generally to Turkish men. Six women had been, or were, married to non-Turks. Many women were pursuing basic literacy training in preparation for the labour market, while others were

Table 5.1. Characteristics of interview subjects

Age	Men	Women
<20		3
20–29	4	22
30–39	2	10
40–49	4	7
>50	—	7
Civil status		
Divorced/separated	7	9
Married	3	37
Engaged	—	3
Background		
Rural area	3	32
Urban area	7	17
Education		
>13 years	8	3
6–12	2	21
1–5	—	18
0	—	7
Occupation		
Teaching	4	5
Student		
Academic level	3	—
Primary school level	—	4
Literacy training	—	4
Translator	1	1
Cleaning/dishwashing	—	18
Cashier	—	2
Self-employed	—	1
Public employee	—	2
Unemployed	2	6
Immigrant status		
First generation	8	30
Second generation	2	19
Total	10	49

generally employed in unqualified service jobs. Some urban educated women were also represented.

At the initial contact, the objective of the study was explained to interview subjects and an attempt was made to collect information on gender and family relations among Turks in Sweden. Anonymity was assured. If the interview subject agreed to participate, an appointment was made and the interviews were carried out, generally in privacy, usually at the interview subject's home (in 6 cases family members wished to listen to the conversation). Eleven women attending courses were interviewed in a separate room at the course locale; five women who had fled from domestic battering were interviewed at a refuge for women.

Interviews were carried out by the author and two experienced Turkish field workers, a man and a woman. The interviewer was generally, but not always, of the same sex as the interviewee. Interviews generally lasted two to three hours (with a range of two to eight hours) and were tape-recorded. The recordings were coded and transcribed, in a slightly edited version.

Each individual was asked to relate his or her life story, including childhood and early school years, adolescence, marriage, family relations and conflicts, and immigration experience, prompted by a set of loosely structured questions. The questionnaire served as a conversational guide; if the interview subject wished to elaborate on his or her feelings and experiences or to discuss a certain conflict area in detail, the conversation was allowed to develop in that direction. People who felt that they had a good understanding of gender and family relations were allowed to give their opinions. Those discussions were sometimes carried out at the expense of other specific areas of discussion in the questionnaire.

The material was qualitatively analysed, focusing on the extent to which gender relations were changing in immigrant families and the factors responsible for the change. Special attention was given to four areas: (1) How much physical, economic, emotional and intellectual autonomy women exercised; (2) To what extent was this autonomy different from patterns in Turkey; (3) How much autonomy was considered acceptable in a foreign country; and, (4) What strategies women use to gain more autonomy in conflict situations.

The study strived to explore the existing cultural themes which define gender relations and their variation. While relating their stories, interview subjects reflected on those aspects of migration which had formed, changed and reshaped their perceptions of gender. They made judgements on the early influences and the new perspectives they had gained. They reflected on those principles they believed were still worth protecting, and explained how they applied these in their daily lives. The exploratory nature of the study allowed for a flexibility which helped to capture the variations on certain cultural themes. An analysis of the material disclosed the different strategies people used for achieving cultural continuity without compromising individual integrity. Two themes in the accounts consistently appeared as culturally important: protection of family unity and sexual honour. These form a cultural consensus for the immigrant group.

Turkish Immigration to Sweden

The Turkish presence in Sweden is not entirely new: two Turks were baptized in 1672 and 1695 at the Nikolai and German Churches, respectively, in Stockholm. Some Ottoman cooks and artisans accompanied Charles XII in 1714 when he returned from Turkey. In the mid-1700s a Turk from Bulgaria travelled north to introduce a certain type of plough to Swedish farmers. At the turn of the twentieth century, there were eight Ottoman Turks in Sweden. In 1950 the number of Turkish citizens had increased to 55 and in 1960, only a few years before the massive immigration boom, the total number was 68 (Svanberg, 1985). In 1987 the number of Turkish citizens in Sweden had reached about 30,000 (including naturalizations and cross-marriages). About a third of these are ethnic Turks; other significant groups are Kurds and Assyrians.

A labour recruitment agreement between Turkey and Sweden was signed in March 1967, but the number of workers who came by virtue of this arrangement was only 331 (Alpay, 1980). The bulk of Turks in Sweden came through chain migration. They arranged jobs through informal channels, mostly private contacts. Six men from Kulu (a town in the province of Konya in central Anatolia) arrived in Sweden to begin working as dishwashers in 1965 (Merdol, 1982). After some time, they helped their relatives and neighbours from the same town to find jobs and emigrate to Sweden. At present, people from Kulu represent the majority of Turks in Sweden. Similar chain migration patterns were established by people in other regions. In addition to labour immigrants, there is a group of Turkish citizens who arrived as political refugees.

Gender Socialization in a European Country

Taking care of children in Turkish culture basically involves feeding them, keeping them clean and protecting them from accidents. These tasks are carried out by mothers or other female kin. Adults generally do not play with children; children play with children, with little supervision from adults.

As the child begins to gain some dexterity, he or she is taught gender-related skills and the process of socialization into gender roles begins. For example, a mother teaches a five-year-old girl how to sew buttons as a game. A farmer's son is trained to capture a chicken for the evening meal. By the time they reach puberty, children have well-defined responsibilities.

A 42-year-old woman:

You follow your mother around and do as she says. In our village a girl must be on her toes all the time. You must jump up and bring water every time somebody is thirsty. You must run every time somebody calls you. You must keep an eye on your brothers and sisters. You must cook and take food to your parents when they are in the fields. It is improper for girls to play as if they were three-year-olds.

A 39-year-old man:

I began work during middle school [ages 12–15]. I began by selling water and soft drinks at the train station. I then became an apprentice at my uncle's carpentry shop, then helped another uncle at his grocery store. Jobs such as working on a chicken farm and running errands at a company followed. On weekends I helped neighbours with building and repairing squatter settlement housing.

Childhood is essentially terminated at between 12 and 14 years of age, around puberty, in many low-income Turkish families.

Circumcision is a practice which reinforces male identification during childhood. In Islamic tradition, boys are circumcised a few years before puberty. Some days before the procedure, a boy is allowed to play with his friends and be as childish as he wishes. He dresses up in a costume: he may be dressed as a prince, an army officer or a fireman. He rides around on horses with his friends, is taken to an amusement park, and so forth. The circumcision ceremony is accompanied by much entertainment. After the medical procedure, he is given presents such as money, a wrist watch or a radio, signifying that he is no longer a little boy. From that time on he becomes a *delikanli* (one with wild blood): he may no longer run to his mother for comfort, weep or be afraid. Any such girlish behaviour would be reprimanded with the reminder that now he must behave like a man.

The corresponding first step to sexual maturity for girls, the beginning of menstruation, is not celebrated. It may even begin with ritual punishment. A practice (which is dying out) is to slap the girl on the face when she tells her mother about her first menstruation. It is reasoned that she is now grown up and must learn not to ask questions about sex (Fahri, 1984).

A 44-year-old woman:

I had not received any information on it [menstruation]. I thought I had some disease. It did not stop. The stain just grew. I showed it to mother in the evening when she came home. She gave me a slap on the face. I didn't know what to do. I began to cry. Mother began to laugh. She laughed and cried at the same time. She then hugged me, started kissing and stroking my hair. She told me what it was. She had made preparations: a dozen small white towels neatly wrapped up in a bundle. She showed me how to take care of myself. She told me she had slapped me so that I would know I was grown up now.

The implications of the rituals for boys and girls are significant: with circumcision a boy enters a period when his blood runs wild – a time when he can be daring and insensitive. With menstruation, a girl enters a period when she must learn not to be proud of her body and not to ask questions about it.

After migration, incomes are seldom generated in the home, in the fields or in a small shop, but rather at some distant, anonymous work place to which adults must go nearly every day, often leaving the children in the care of unrelated people. Urban homes become primarily a place for recreation where only a portion of the day is spent. Securing the livelihood of the family becomes a strictly adult responsibility. The contribution of children is no longer necessary, so they are not taught gender-related skills and responsibilities to the same extent as rural Turkish children. The degree of early gender identification decreases. Childhood is prolonged.

A 22-year-old woman:

> Our oldest sister had to do a lot of work at home because we had just migrated to Sweden and there was nobody to take care of us. She could never begin working outside our home. She still sits at home. I was not expected to do much housework until I got married. I wish I had been asked to help. Housework seemed so difficult later on.

Western child care and educational institutions encourage children to develop their individual capacities under non-authoritarian conditions. This contributes to a prolongation of childhood with minimal gender identification. Gender differences are de-emphasized. Children receive factual information on sexuality. As such, it is very different from the environment in which children acquire Turkish-style gender identification in the home country.

A 44-year-old woman:

> Our 13-year-old daughter built a lamp stand as a present for us on our wedding anniversary. They teach girls metal work and carpentry at school, while boys take lessons in sewing and cooking. I hear that boys sew karate overalls for themselves. Karate or not, they sew! Imagine this happening in Turkey!

As puberty approaches, parents realize that their children have developed many individualistic attitudes that do not conform with their own conception of childhood.

A Turkish male school teacher explains:

> Teachers and parents do not have as much authority as in Turkey. Children do not learn to respect elders: they become much too individualistic. Parents cannot be strict. Youngsters actually know they can complain and receive support from authorities if their parents domineer too much. They get their way. What is especially frightening for Turkish parents is that early experimentation with sexuality is possible. Girls can begin having boyfriends, dressing like adults and going out at night when they are 13 or 14 years old. It seems unacceptable, very threatening to parents.

The struggle to give children growing up in Western society a Turkish–Muslim gender identity often begins at this relatively late stage, when children have developed a number of independent personality characteristics. Many parents are unprepared for the task. They do not have the time, the pedagogical competence, sufficient understanding of the Western youth culture, or the reasons underlying their own traditions. Their approach can be too generalized and authoritarian.

A 28-year-old woman reflects on her childhood and the attitudes of her parents:

> They just said no, you can't do this or that. Nothing more! When we asked why, they would say: 'Such is our tradition, such is our religion.' But, 'Why, why?' we would ask. And they would say, 'It is a matter of honour. You may not shame our family. People will talk.'

Complaints are sometimes made at schools about the sex education curriculum. Teachers are asked not to allow mixed-gender children groups to sit together. The pressure is mostly on girls. Their participation in certain activities, such as gymnastics, swimming and dancing may be banned by their families. Even though families do not pressure the girls to cover their hair, they are required to wear 'decent', unsuggestive clothes, and to come directly home from school. Few girls are allowed to go anywhere with their friends after dark (Yazgan, 1983).

Children are encouraged to take Koran courses where much emphasis is given to gender segregation, the necessity for obedience, family honour and shame. Many children begin study but most drop out after some months of attendance. Parents do not pursue the issue.

A 36-year-old mother:

> I wanted my children to take Koran courses, so they can learn about our traditions. Both of them wanted to attend but it did not go very well. Children these days cannot sit still. I think the courses were too difficult. A lot of memorizing. The girl went for four months. The boy went only twice. Then they lost interest. I did not want to force them. You cannot force religion. They should not resent religious learning.

Adolescence

Most men in Turkey acquire their first sexual experience by visiting prostitutes. Each town or city has its bordello, which is run as a legal enterprise. It is called a 'public house'; women who work there are 'public women'. It is an accepted practice that a boy who has come of age be invited by an uncle, an older brother or some friends to make a first visit. Some men take the experience for granted; for others it may be traumatic (Månsson, 1984).

This pattern changes significantly in Swedish society, where boys have their early sexual experiences with Western girls in the same age group. The girls are not prostitutes, but family girls, as they are called in Turkish. The boys develop double standards. Coming from a culture where pre-marital and extra-marital experience of women (particularly young girls) is strongly stigmatized, for many it becomes difficult to define the nature of their sexual contacts with Western girls.

A 20-year-old man:

> It is hard to really trust foreign girls. You can never know what is going on in their heads. They have had relationships before you, and you want to forget them, but that they may have a relationship after you, that they may even be having a relationship when they are with you, makes you uncertain about what you are worth for her.

The tendency is for boys and young men to have many short-term relationships, yet they long for something more meaningful (Månsson, 1984). There is much insecurity and confusion. Degrading or defensive attitudes develop in the men. Aronowitz (1988) describes the attitudes of young Turkish men in Germany, which are typical of immigrant Turks.

> The most striking thing about the youth clubs, in which interviews were conducted, was that the participants were predominantly [Turkish] male youths. In some of the clubs, there were a few German male or female youths, but rarely were Turkish female youths to be seen. When asked about this, the youths replied that their sisters were forbidden to attend such youth clubs because of the number of male youths found there. They themselves would forbid their sisters to attend if their parents did not. When asked the question concerning girls having relationships with boys before marriage and whether or not they can thereby earn respect, a large percentage replied negatively (45%). A small percentage of the interviewed youth remarked that if they ever learned that their sisters were having a sexual relationship before she was married, they would kill her. The sexual act would bring dishonour to the family. This held true for Turkish females. A double standard applied to the sexual behaviour of male youths as well as German females (29% of the sample replied that their response to the question would depend on whether the girl was German or Turkish). Interestingly enough, many of the youths interviewed reported having sexual relations, but almost exclusively with German or other foreign girls, not with Turkish girls. When asked if they would ever marry a German girl, 36% of the youths replied negatively. Their reason for such a reply was found in their conviction that German girls were not 'pure'. . . . The question concerning family honour is of interest. Almost half of the sample (50%) felt obliged to attack a person who jeopardizes the honour of the family. Another 10% felt that one should react in that way. While 31.5% felt that such an action was dependent upon the situation, only 8.5% felt that this type of aggressive behaviour was unjustifiable.

Turkish girls are expected not to have any pre-marital sexual experience. Adolescence is the time when marriage becomes an issue for girls, at home or abroad. Early marriage is characteristic of most rural and low-income communities; the Islamic rejection of celibacy and pre-marital relations is also a factor in the early marriage of girls. It is considered cruel to force youths into celibacy by letting them remain unmarried during adolescence. The only exception is youths, usually boys, who are pursuing studies or careers. In order to delay a marriage, a girl must be exceptionally good at her studies or have the support of liberal parents.

A 42-year-old woman, the daughter of a wealthy family from a city, explains her parents' reasoning when her marriage was arranged at the age of 17:

> My father initially was hopeful that I would continue my studies – he wanted me to become a lawyer like himself. Unfortunately, my average grades at school fell in the eighth grade and I failed in six courses the next year. You know how it is – youth, dreams. I couldn't concentrate on my studies. Two boys were in love with me; they were sending secret letters, following me in the streets and so forth. I felt flattered. I was having a lot of fun, but people in town had begun talking. My failing in my lessons was like the last straw – they reasoned that since I was so pretty, men would not leave me alone, and that I would go bad. So they decided I should get married.

It is believed that an attractive young girl is so appealing that men will pursue her relentlessly. Because a woman's sexual needs are so strong, it is feared that she will sooner or later respond to suggestion, leading to an illicit sexual relationship. A succinct Turkish saying is: 'A girl should be married before she opens her eyes.' A young woman must be secured in marriage before she gains too much experience and threatens to bring shame to her family.

Marriage partners with residence and work permits in a European country are extremely attractive. The families of boys still in Turkey are willing to pay a high price for a Turkish bride living in Europe. Likewise, an emigrant boy is such a desirable groom that a girl's family may give their daughter for a very small bride-price. Even when no bride-price is involved, marriage with an immigrant Turk will be economically advantageous. Families may also arrange marriages to repay favours or strengthen bonds.

Second generation Turks are questioning early arranged marriages; boys and girls are resisting it for different reasons. For boys, the idea of marrying someone their parents have chosen is disturbing because of possible physical incompatibility. Boys are otherwise conservative about gender roles and generally agree with traditional male privileges. They do not think early marriage would necessarily upset their daily routines or life plans and it does not. For women, however, resistance to early arranged marriage is of vital importance. They are aware that physical or intellectual incompatibility with their spouses would not only threaten their emotional stability, but would jeopardize their integration into the labour market. The traditional extended family structure is breaking down in favour of the nuclear family. A nuclear family does not have a large number of other people to whom an individual can turn for help; it has only two adults who must help and support each other in every way. It is necessary for the adults to be able to communicate with each other across the gender barrier. Young women, more often than men, sense that gender role-sharing is vitally important to enable them to carry out the double workload in a nuclear family. The young women's arguments against an early arranged marriage with an incompatible spouse are consistent and logical: they want to marry men with whom they can become good companions.

A 28-year-old woman:

> Stockholm is not Kulu. You cannot let the kids run around in the back garden when you work. Nobody takes care of them. You must send them to a day nursery. You must pay for that. Men cannot sit at the coffee shop six months a year and manage to bring home bread. You cannot feed a family on even one person's salary. If the wife is going to work, if she is going to bring home a salary, then she needs some help with the house. She will not put up with a husband puffing cigarettes on the couch. Salary like salary. Work like work.
>
> My mother worked as a cleaner and was responsible for all the housework and taking care of us five children. She gave all her salary to father and he bought property in Turkey. She is now unable to work because of her back. She has never complained. But I was not going to allow this to happen to me. I did not want to marry and serve a man and break my back just because he was a man, without even getting a bit of attention or recognition.

Nevertheless this woman did get married in her teens against her will. Some years afterwards she left her husband, moved to another city, finished primary school (*grundskola*), remarried, had a child, divorced once again, obtained occupational training and is presently employed as a qualified worker. Her motives, typical of many girls who want to be able to select their own future husbands, are not romantic, but logical: there must be compatibility and respect, otherwise the burden will become impossible to bear.

An 18-year-old who convinced her parents to let her make her own choice about marriage:

> I simply threatened them with running away. I said, 'If you don't let me know him properly before we are married – I promise not to do anything bad – I will surely find a way to run away from you and from him, and you will never see me again.' They got very upset. Father's face turned red as a beet. Mother almost got up to hit me. But what could they do? Then I said, 'If I like him, I will get engaged, but I don't want to get married before I finish school because I want to get a good job.' They grumbled and mumbled. Fortunately the boy they found is really nice. He is a student in Turkey. When we are in Turkey, we meet. He takes me out to tea. I tell him about life in Sweden. We write letters to each other. I tell him I want a good job. First I will finish school, then I will begin work, save money and find an apartment. Then we get married and he comes here. He says 'Yes, yes!'

To avoid parental pressure in Turkey, girls elope with a boy of their choice. This does not break the basic pattern of moving from the paternal home to a husband's home. A realistic girl in Turkey does not have the option of leaving her parental home to live alone. Neither can she threaten her parents with such plans. The number of girls who abandon their families to live alone in Europe is increasing which, considering the implications for family honour, is a source of great anxiety for parents. Knowing this, some girls dare to threaten their parents with running away to build a life on their own terms; a few actually leave. The consequences, however, are heavy. Ties with the family and the Turkish community may be irreparably broken. Isolation and loneliness follow. Both parties are careful to avoid such a drastic occurrence. Parents often yield to the wishes of their daughters as they strive for more autonomy, within the limits of honour.

Marriage

Marriage partners from Turkey are more desirable than foreigners or Turks living in Europe. It is difficult for immigrant Turks to find spouses during the short visits they make to Turkey. Others are expected to help by searching for suitable future spouses and introducing them to one other, hence marriages are still arranged. This is different to the traditional early arranged marriage in that the couple have the opportunity to meet several times before getting married, and feel free to refuse the selected partner if they wish. The couple get married after a relatively short period of acquaintanceship. Their knowledge of each other is rarely intimate. About a third of marriages are between cousins or other relatives; most marriages are with people from the same village or town.

Most commonly the bride from Turkey joins her husband's parental household in Europe. The couple are generally too young and financially too weak to establish a separate household. The bride's situation is comparable to that of many newly married couples in Turkey: she lives with the husband's parents and pools income until the bride-price and wedding expenses are repaid and money is saved to establish a new household. This is, in many ways, the most difficult situation in which a young woman can find herself. She must not only adjust to marital life with her husband, but also to his family. Furthermore, she is living in a new, foreign country. Frequently her status in her husband's family is low. She must learn about the household conventions and be ready to serve everybody. She must prove her fertility by having a baby as soon as possible. She may be required to take on outside work. Her adjustment to her new environment proceeds under the close supervision of her mother-in-law who, more often than not, recreates the conditions of her own indoctrination as a bride. Unlike in Turkey, the immigrant bride may not have any blood relatives to turn to in the foreign country. Neither may she expect automatic support and understanding from her husband: he would hesitate to defend his wife against demands from his parents, particularly while he and his wife are still sharing their residence.

A Turkish social worker explains:

> Most of all I pity the village girls who marry into families with a hurricane mother-in-law. The brides are usually very young and inexperienced. The

marriage does not in any way inconvenience their husbands. The men go on living with their parents, they know Western society, they have their friends and they even maintain their non-Turkish female acquaintances. The man's family does not place any demands on him. Men have all the freedom on earth. On top of that, they have a nice, clean woman at home serving them and their family, giving them children and even working and putting money in their pocket. How different it is for the girl! Coming to such a different environment. She does not know what should have first priority: serve her husband, serve his family, please the mother-in-law, learn to cook, learn to take care of children, learn an occupation, learn a language, learn new ways and values. . . . Through all of this she has minimal support!

A 25-year-old:

The period of living with my mother-in-law was worst. I was 18 when I came [to Sweden]. I was expecting a life like those on TV. In Turkey you think Europe is something. You think people live like kings. I arrived only to find an overcrowded apartment and a very cold, dark country. I became a servant in the family. Two children, a teenage brother-in-law and parents-in-law in four rooms! I who had been my father's favourite child! I who was not required to do anything at home! I used to think of home, and weep. If father had seen me then. A job was already arranged for me: cleaning a day nursery in the evenings. I had to serve all day and worked at night. I could not take care of my babies myself; my mother-in-law took care of them and sent me off to cook, to clean, to work.

Another arrangement is that the groom arrives from Turkey and joins the family of his wife. This situation is more favourable for the wife, but the husband may feel alienated.

The social worker:

It is then a different story. This time it is the wife and her family who have the upper hand; the wife takes over the role of initiator of her husband into Sweden. She helps him with contacts, finding a job, learning the language, and so forth. The husband enters the social circle of the girl's family. It is a delicate situation. The male image being what it is in our culture, it is easy to end up with a resentful husband and a mocking wife. It does have its complications.

A 45-year-old mother disapprovingly recounts how her daughter became a 'mocking wife':

At first she liked her husband, but things changed after he came here. We brought her up liberally. No pressure. She is like a Swedish girl. But the groom is a Turkish man. Our men are jealous. She would not let him open his mouth! How very embarrassing! He would tell her not to wear something and she would say, 'Hush, what do you know, peasant!' He would ask her to bring a glass of water, and she would say, 'Go get it yourself!' That is no way to treat a husband. Then she wanted to sleep separately. She wanted to divorce him, to send him back to Turkey. God knows, I feel terribly embarrassed. The groom is my sister's husband's nephew. I keep telling her, you must respect your husband, you are his honour; of course he is going to be jealous of you, but does she listen to me? No!

Most wives and their families, however, are sensitive to the groom's predicament, and try not to hurt his sense of male pride.

A 28-year-old second generation woman, presently employed as a professional, tells her story:

We had to live with my parents for about two years after the wedding for economic reasons. We were all very careful. My parents gave us their bedroom, sleeping in the living room so we would have some privacy. Mother was very careful that my husband would not exploit me, but at the same time that he would feel like a man. For instance she would prepare breakfast for us before going to work so as to make the point that I needed my sleep; neither did she want him to do any housework in her home. My family did not let us make any monetary contribution; we saved for ourselves. Thanks to that, we were able to move out soon.

He was a little aggressive in the first years. I did not tell my parents about it, or they would have forced us to divorce. I understood his aggression; he feels inferior, or less than manly, or something. Although he had a good education in Turkey, he did not manage to learn Swedish very well. He works in a factory and says he likes it. I, of course, speak better Swedish and have a high status job. I am careful about this. He never asks, and I never tell him about the very exciting things I am doing at my job. When he says he likes his job, I never chide him to learn more Swedish and get a better job. We usually just talk about the children. He sometimes gets jealous, tells me not to wear make-up, or something. Then I don't wear make-up. What do I need make-up for?

Newly-weds occasionally move into their own home at the beginning of their marriage. People, usually men, who do not have a large family or who are older or divorced, start a nuclear family. Excluding educated or divorced women, there are relatively few single Turkish women who establish separate households.

The power relationship in a nuclear household is determined by the length of stay in Europe; the spouse who knows the Western lifestyle best becomes the decision-maker.

A 33-year-old woman reflects on how her husband was established as the decision-maker in her marriage:

A divorced man and I met three or four times to have tea. He told me all about his life. He had been married once and had lived with another woman. Both women were non-Turks. He had three children who lived with their mothers. He had lived in Europe for 20 years. He was an architect, he said, an interior decorator. He was dark, good-looking and sensitive. He said he longed for a Turkish wife. I liked him. I was 19, he was 32. We were married within three weeks. No bride-price was paid.

I was amazed with Sweden; such a clean country. Calm, good-looking people, always smiling. My husband's house was very nice. Two rooms and a large kitchen. Continuously running water. Both hot and cold. A refrigerator and a freezer. A vacuum cleaner. Shops full of merchandise.

Now we have two children. It turned out that he was not an architect but a painter. He paints walls and window frames. He earns well. He does not want me to work. He says he wants a lady in his house. Unfortunately I cannot speak Swedish. I did not go to any courses. I understand the language, but I cannot speak. It may sound strange, because I have an education and have lived in Sweden for 14 years. Sometimes I suspect my children are ashamed of me. When they bring their friends home, I cannot say anything but 'Hej, välkommen' (hello, welcome). Maybe, in a couple of years, we will return to Turkey, where my husband says I will not need to be ashamed of anything.

A woman in her late twenties, who took the initiative to remarry, discloses her own primacy in decision-making:

I began feeling lonely some time after the divorce. A woman cannot live alone and children need a father. [She refuses to let her ex-husband see the children.] I wrote to my mother in the village and told her to arrange a marriage for me. I told her I wanted to marry a poor fatherless person, like myself. [Her father died when she was young.] I told her I don't want him to pay a bride-price, but he must accept my children and be like a father to them. She arranged for me to marry my present husband. He is from another village. He is ten years older than me. He is very poor. I am his second wife. His first wife abandoned him for someone else, leaving him with three children. He told my mother he would not mind my children. He even said he would leave his own children in the village, if I would have him. I went to the country, we got married and I brought him here. He left his children with his sister. We send them money. He works at the same restaurant as I. I told my boss that I now have a husband who needs a job, and the boss hired him. We wash dishes, both of us. We earn well.

He sometimes gets dreamy and I know he is thinking of his children. In a way, I think, his children are orphans. Their mother ran away, their father left them. You don't have to die to leave children as orphans, do you? He has accepted my children, so I am thinking that perhaps we should send for his children.

If it is the husband who knows Europe best, his role as decision-maker is unquestioned. A wife who knows the host country better than her husband can, however, enjoy considerable prerogatives in decision-making, from the beginning of the relationship.

Immigrant Turks also marry other immigrants, usually non-Turks (a discussion of mixed-ethnic marriages is beyond the scope of this study). There are more such marriages among Turkish men; very few Turkish women enter mixed marriages. Marriages between Turks settled in Europe are also few and occur mostly among well-educated Turks.

When the enormous adjustments to a new marriage have been made, the couple settles into a more or less stable routine of roles and responsibilities that have been re-defined to suit the demands of life in a foreign country. Besides the changing methods of child-rearing (Ergun-Engström and Heyman, 1989), there is a redefinition of roles when women begin working outside the home, and in the division of household responsibilities.

Women's employment

When men first brought their wives and children to Europe, the issue of whether or not the women should be allowed to work outside the home had to be confronted. One of the earliest immigrant workers from Kulu recounts the concerns:

> When I told my father and the village elders about my plan [to take my wife to Sweden], they all stood up, and asked, 'What? Take a woman to an infidel country? What about our honour?' I laughed at them and I said, 'This is not a matter of honour. She is still my wife and I am still a Muslim. But I will take her and I will let her work if she wishes.' They said: 'You must be out of your mind! How are you going to let your woman work side-by-side with men in a foreign land?'

Women's outside employment implied a temporary relinquishing of community control as women travelled to and from the workplace and mingled with strangers. Women would be learning new skills and values; they would be earning cash for their labour. All this would contribute to increased female autonomy which – if it got out of hand – would threaten the family honour and tradition. But the additional income was needed. The solution was to extend social control to the workplace.

One measure was a purposeful search for gender-segregated jobs, or jobs where a woman would be working by herself, with other women or with her husband. In the UK and France, Turkish women take piece-work in their homes. In West Germany, many women work as domestic servants. The most 'proper' jobs for Turkish women in Scandinavia are referred to as 'key-jobs' – whereby the woman is given a door key for entering and cleaning a building after normal work hours. Women so employed are isolated from foreign influence. The second preference is for jobs where other Turks work. Teams of Turkish women are established at factories and other workplaces which employ largely female labour. To work outside the home, women must gain the confidence of men. They do this by becoming conservative judges of other women and keeping a sharp eye on one another, exerting effective social control at the workplace. A woman comments:

I don't blame men as much as I blame women. Men are men. They are sensitive about matters of honour; it is their upbringing; they have it in their system; they can't help it. Whatever. But women! It is they who, with their vicious gossip, bring misfortune to themselves. Take our workplace, for instance. Naime Hanum behaves as if she were everybody's mother-in-law. The slightest false step, and that night everybody in the neighbourhood hears about it. The other day Mehmet's wife went to the hospital coffee shop with a [non-Turkish] girlfriend. They just went to have coffee, you know. And this non-Turkish girl's boyfriend and some other men joined them there and Mehmet's wife could not just jump up and run away from them, could she? We Turkish women have already become a laughing stock for being as shy and jumpy as we are. She just sat with them and finished her coffee. So what is so wrong about that? Believe me, that night, everybody had heard what had happened. Mehmet's wife meets men. Mehmet's wife is Westernized. Smiles, meaningful looks. . . . Of course her husband gets upset!

Control by the older women and the mother-in-law in a Turkish village household extends to the workplace in Europe. Turkish women judge each other's behaviour in public in Europe. Age and seniority is replaced by the degree of conservativeness. Gossip is used as an effective tool for social control.

This conservatism in judging other women is not absolute or consistent. Many women have begun to reflect on the female condition and question traditional mores. Attitudes towards the gender-related behaviour of the closest women kin – daughters and sisters – become more tolerant. Some change occurs with opposition, such as the resistance of daughters to covering their hair or to early arranged marriage. Much change has sprung from a desire for less social control; complaints about gossip are widespread.

The income a woman generates through outside employment does not lead directly to economic independence or increased autonomy. Her income is given initially to her father-in-law and later to her husband, and is used according to their wishes. As is true of women in Turkey, employed immigrant women give priority to their roles as mothers and wives above their jobs. This is true even when they are the sole breadwinners of the family for long periods. Many women perceive their work and income, in the long term, as being insignificant. A young woman who gave up studies to support her husband during his university studies, comments:

I think it is vulgar to differentiate between my income and your income. It is our income, no matter who brings it in. I bring it in today, when he is studying. He will bring it in tomorrow, and it will be more than I could ever earn. Women cannot ever earn as much as men, not if they want a family and children. My contribution is temporary. His will be permanent.

A woman's attitude towards the contribution of her job is more positive when it carries the promise of intellectual stimulation and advancement which, unfortunately, is rarely the case for immigrants ('Raise your voice', 1985, Stiver Lie, 1985). Employment is desirable because it allows women to emerge from the isolation of a suburban immigrant apartment building. It becomes meaningful if and when it changes the traditional female self-image. As in the home country, immigrant Turkish women tend to show increased independence from traditional mores as they improve their educational and occupational status. This was observed in most accounts given by women in this study.

The following is a summary of how a 46-year-old woman's progression from an unqualified to a qualified job changed her outlook:

> I was suspicious when I started taking those courses. I was temporarily unemployed, so I started taking them just to pass time and earn some money. I did not really think I could learn to read and write in Turkish. I did not think it was necessary for me as a woman, in fact. I was over 30 years old at the time. I used to laugh at myself when I found myself sitting there like a little child with a pencil and alphabet. It was very hard in the beginning. I could not understand the teachers or even hold a pencil right. After some months I began reading syllables; then I began reading my children's homework and Turkish newspapers. That was long ago. Now I read pretty well. I read everything. I get letters from the country and write back. Before, I used to depend on my children for writing or reading letters. . . . Learning to read and write Turkish helped me learn Swedish. You cannot capture what people say if you cannot see the words. When you can read, you begin seeing the words in the captions of newspapers, under TV films, on road signs. Then you remember the words. I now speak quite a bit of Swedish. When you speak Swedish, you get along better with your boss. Your friends respect you. Now I am studying to become a child-care assistant. I support the education of girls. In the country they ask, 'What is a girl going to do with an education?' She can work and be respected, that's what she can do! She can make herself heard! But who wants that? A girl is not supposed to open her eyes in Turkey. My girls studied. I kept telling them to study as much as they could while they had the opportunity. Education is almost more important for girls.

It is questionable if this woman would have made these last statements if she had continued in her unqualified job which brought her an income, but no prospects for advancement. Each step forward in educational and occupational status, not matter how small, is always followed by an increased sense of personal worth and more ambitious plans for the future. The key to emancipation lies in career orientation and professionalism – not in the salary!

Household responsibilities

In Western societies, when both spouses have jobs outside the home, sharing housework is perceived as role sharing. First-generation Turkish immigrants who have a very strong gender role identification do not share housework. Generally, women do not demand that they do and men would not tolerate it if they did. After migration, many women find their workload considerably decreased. Heavy tasks, such as working in the fields, taking care of animals, carrying water, preparing and storing food for winter, and sewing clothes are no longer necessary. Others, such as doing the laundry and cleaning floors, are facilitated by machines. Summers in European cities are not as dusty, and winters not as muddy, as they are in Turkish villages. Immigrant Turkish homes have simple furnishings that need minimal care. In countries with good child care facilities, the young children and most other family members are away from home most of the day. Housework, which is considered unimportant in rural Turkey, becomes even more insignificant. A woman comments:

> I would never let my husband or sons work in the house. What are we women for? These new women want their men to help out. We don't. It is not in our tradition. Besides, what is housework in Sweden, compared to Turkey! Here you do everything with machines. I don't call that work.

Her phrase 'what are we women for?' summarizes an attitude: as in Turkey, women attempt to solve by themselves the problems created by the double workload, without placing demands on their men. Daughters and brides are called upon for help as an ageing woman begins to retire from work.

Second-generation girls find it unfair that they are expected to do so much housework while their brothers are allowed to be idle. These girls say they will expect their future husbands to help with the housework. Role-sharing is the second generation's most important expectation from a successful marriage, even more important than that for romance. Men are, however, often unwilling or unable to help. Turkish women, with their great talent for adaptability, adjust by rationalizing.

> I feel uneasy when he begins helping me. He is sloppy. I often have to go over what he has done and make it right. If I tell him to do it right, he gets angry and says I should not give orders. Arguing is too much trouble. I just fix it myself, very quickly.
>
> People make a great fuss over helping with housework. It is as if everything in a marriage depends on who washes the dishes. Buy a machine and let it wash the dishes! Strange reasoning! Washing dishes shouldn't be an issue so big that it threatens a marriage.

Second-generation men and those from towns and cities take pride in saying they help their wives. Some of them take over tasks which are glamorous to the migrant: cooking ethnic dishes or playing with the children and taking them out. The husbands of women working at odd hours take care of the children if there is no other alternative. Women are thankful for, and proud of, any help they get.

He is very considerate. If he thinks I look tired, he tells me to rest and fixes the dinner. He does not nag or sulk as some men do. He does not mind serving the tea when we have guests. He takes the children out whenever the weather is good and on other occasions.

First and second generation Turkish immigrant men take responsibility for the family in public affairs not involving children, while women take care of the home and children (Similä, 1987). Only a handful of educated urban women participate in the organized activities of immigrants on an equal footing with men. Women with traditional backgrounds rarely participate in any type of political or cultural activity where there is a significant male representation. An urban woman with many years of experience in cultural organizations explains:

> First-generation women generally do not come to public meetings. Some would come if accompanied by their men, but then they come as spectators; they do not participate. Even women whom I know have a lot of ideas and would speak up if they were among women, get very quiet in public, in the presence of their own men. It is because of the tradition of letting men represent them in public. There is some pressure from the men too, I think. Men seem not to mind hearing the opinions of other women, but get very embarrassed if the woman who steps forward is in some way related to them. We women with education are often compelled to speak for traditional women. This sometimes creates awkward situations, because the socio-cultural distance between village and city in Turkey is as great as the distance between Turkey and Sweden. We are not good representatives for traditional women, really.

A significant change has occurred in terms of representing the family in interactions with the public institutions of the host country. Women, in many instances, are the initiators of contact with the authorities in areas such as health insurance, child care, school and housing (Kudat and Frey, 1975; Mortensen, 1989). It is felt that Turkish women are dealt with more sympathetically and that their needs are taken more seriously.

A Turkish social worker explains:

> People don't say it in so many words, but men are definitely discriminated against in certain situations. If a Turkish woman loses her job, for instance, it is assumed that it must have happened because of some pressing problem she could not handle, and everybody is eager to help her. A man in her situation would also be helped, but perhaps without similar commitment. Women's needs are given priority in a variety of situations. Perhaps there is a need for doing so, I don't know. There is a preference to let women handle the contacts with authorities in the belief that they will receive more effective help.

A 36-year-old woman offers a different perspective:

It is better that women contact the authorities. Most of the people working there are women. Women understand you better when you go and tell them your children need a place at day care so you can work, or when you say you need a bigger apartment. Women also work at hospitals and clinics, so it is better if I, instead of my husband, take the children for health care. My husband would not know how to discuss matters about home and children with a woman. He would forget what the doctors say about the child's health. I follow up on such matters.

The later years of marriage

As the years of marriage advance, the woman's role gradually changes from that of the marginal bride to the central, all-important mother. It is she who, during many years of quiet service, has kept the family together. Meanwhile, the 'wild-blooded', powerful husband and father, as he ages, becomes somewhat marginalized.

A 32-year-old man describes his father's old age with pity:

We feared father. There was not much we could discuss or do together. I remember speaking to him only for money or to get permission for something. I don't know why the relationship was so restrained; it was not that our father was a terribly domineering person, or anything like that. I now feel sorry for him, a little bit. Imagine what he must have gone through! Leaving your village, coming to a Nordic country, the humiliation, the loneliness. . . . How I hoped they could return to Turkey. Now they can't return because many of their friends and relatives in the village have died, and we are staying here. If they had returned, father would maybe have been able to relive his youth.

The mother has kept the family intact. As such, she promotes cultural continuity, representing a conservative, protective force as the controller of girls and other women. It may seem paradoxical to find some of these older women now making bold decisions. A 62-year-old woman, who made such a decision, explains:

He had been talking about returning to the village for several years. Then he started making preparations: he bought a new car, paid debts, transferred money to Turkey, arranged papers with the embassy. I said nothing, just watched him. It was amusing. Then one day he came to me and told me to pack because we were leaving in two weeks. I said, 'Goodbye to you. I shall not pack, because I am not going back.' He couldn't believe his ears! He said, 'What do you mean, you're not coming? We decided to return years ago!' I said, 'That was your decision. I had no such intention but you never asked my opinion. No, I shall not return to the village. My children are here, I have my pension, I am comfortable. I don't want to return to the village to all that housework. Goodbye to you!'

Her husband did not – could not – return to the village without his wife. Another older woman briefly relates the story of her marital years:

> For years I put up with everything: his mother, his girlfriends, his gambling and violence. [I told myself] it was a matter of honour; it was for the sake of the children. I put up with all this, but now I am old and cannot tolerate any more disrespect. Thank God the children are grown up and have their own homes. Two years ago he came home from visiting his mistress and was disrespectful again. I called my oldest son and told him to take his father away. The next day I changed the lock to our apartment. He tried to force his way in a couple of times, but I called my sons to take him away. He is now living with his girlfriend. We are divorced. I am, for the first time in my life, at leisure.

As her physical attractiveness decreases and her reproductive years end, an older women is freed of the conventions surrounding the protection of honour. She commands considerable respect and affection from her adult children. She has learned to exercise self-control and independent judgement during her years of employment and she realizes that she no longer needs the financial support of a husband or sons for survival: an older woman often becomes more self-reliant.

Problem areas

Battering

Domestic violence exists in nearly all societies. The Turkish family is no exception. According to a survey carried out in Istanbul, 29% of Turkish women have, some time in their life or routinely, experienced violence within the family (*Bagir, herkes duysun*, 1988). It is not possible to give an accurate figure on the extent of domestic violence among immigrant Turks, but it is thought to be common. Researchers and volunteers working with battered women concur that a large proportion of women who seek medical treatment and refuge from battering are immigrants (Bergman, 1987). About half of all women who seek help at the Stockholm House for Women have immigrant backgrounds (personal communication).

These anecdotes are mentioned in passing:

> I had to come home directly. Mother would otherwise complain to my brothers and they would punish me.

> I refused to sleep with this boy for some months after we got married. He complained to my parents, and they called my brother, and he hit me and ordered me to sleep with my husband.

> He was a little aggressive in the beginning. I did not tell my family about it.

For years I put up with everything: his mother, his girlfriends, his gambling, his beating.

Some men justify the violence they inflict on women.

In the village it is almost high status for a woman to go around with a black eye every now and then. It is believed that men beat their women in passion. Men beat the women they are jealous of, that they care about. Women are proud of being beaten by their men.

This rationale is not true. Women are not proud of being beaten by men. Some feel helpless and put up with it, in the hope that someday the beatings will stop. Others are physically or psychologically maimed.

Parental physical punishment may be tolerated because of the respect (and affection) parents command. It is believed that a parent (or other family member, such as a brother, who acts with parental permission) would usually not resort to violence unless there is good reason. The physical damage is seldom severe; family members set limits. Women say they are sometimes battered by their husbands for no apparent reason:

It was not only when he was jealous. It could happen any time, for any reason. Like, maybe my not having cooked a soup well, or not having emptied an ashtray would be a reason. Once, when walking in the street. I was struck because I tripped and almost fell down. He grabbed me by the arm, and the next thing I knew, I was hit in the face. He shouted at me to be careful when I walk!

Some women may see the battering as a period they must go through until the man feels secure in his role as a husband:

He was aggressive in the beginning. His life was very difficult. He wanted to show that he was the boss in his home. I usually found a way to run out of the apartment, to the neighbours. Then he would come and take me back. We had become a theatre piece in the apartment building! He then would be very remorseful. He would apologize and weep. That period is over now. I am older.

Most women feel compelled to put up with it as they see no alternative other than divorce, which they want to avoid if possible. Many women get very little support or understanding from their relatives once a pattern of battering has been established:

My sisters-in-law kept telling me to be patient. Once I escaped, but I came back. They were angry at me for having deserted my husband. One of them said, 'Who are you to complain about your husband! Do you think you are some kind of a princess? Why can't you put up with something we all have to go through?'

I ran away to my parents and stayed there for a month. My parents in the beginning were on my side. After a while, however, they began telling me to go back, that I belonged where my husband was, that husbands are such that they 'both love and hit'.

The five women in this study who had taken refuge in a shelter for battered women were helped by someone outside their circle of closest acquaintances:

A non-Turkish friend from my workplace kept asking about my bruises. One day I told her all about it. She said I must complain. I knew I should complain, but I did not know how. She told me she would help me the next time it happened. It happened again soon enough, within a few days. I secretly took a few clothes with me that morning as I left for work. We asked for permission from the boss: my friend went with me to the police. Then we went to a hospital, and got a doctor's report. Finally, my friend brought me to the women's house.

The translator who was called to the hospital told me not to go back; that there was a house for women, that she would take me there after I visited the hospital, that I should not be afraid, that he would not be able to find me.

Domestic violence in Turkish immigrant families is sometimes explained as being the result of the emasculating effect of a foreign environment, whereby men feel they have no control over their lives. It is seen as a desperate attempt by men to regain control of their lives. Although there is some truth in this explanation, it does not offer a solution to the women who are suffering.

Divorce
Despite its liberal divorce law, Turkey has one of the lowest divorce rates in the world. For Turks, divorce is a drastic measure to be employed only in extreme situations. The only justifiable reason for a man to seek divorce is his wife's adultery or sterility, and for a woman, extreme financial neglect or physical cruelty by the husband.

Women who seek divorce with insufficient reason are stigmatized. As homemakers and mothers, they should, it is felt, have been patient: men have crises that eventually pass and then they come home. Men whose wives seek divorces are also subject to society's criticism. They are suspected of being intolerable to live with – which, no doubt, they are – since a woman with good judgement would never want a divorce.

Life becomes very difficult for a divorced woman. No longer a virgin, she is considered a candidate for illicit sexual adventures. Those who lack income and education have no means of supporting themselves and their children in Turkey where unemployment is high. Some women may have sexual relationships in exchange for maintenance, although this is rare: honour is all too important. Some divorcées become domestic servants. The majority are compelled to return to their parental home to await remarriage as soon as possible.

It is difficult to quantify the divorce rate of Turks living in Europe. Official statistics show that Turkish citizens have the lowest divorce rate of the immigrant population, but it is high compared to rates in Turkey. Immigrant women who have an independent income are able to keep their children and establish a separate home. But they risk losing family support, and often become outcasts in the Turkish community. They invite a life of isolation and alienation in a foreign country with few prospects for companionship or remarriage. Divorce remains the most drastic measure for women who are involved in a difficult marriage, but it is on the increase, especially among the second generation. The strategy of getting out of an arranged marriage is used as much by men as women. It can create complications.

A 24-year-old woman describes how her strategy worked:

I thought I would marry him to satisfy my parents and get a divorce afterwards. I was young and I thought it would be easy. He is related to us. We moved into my mother's home. I did not like him at all. They sensed that I would want a divorce. My brothers kept a sharp eye on me so I would not run away. If I applied for divorce during the first two years he would be sent back to Turkey, and that would bring shame to my family. Mother wanted me to get pregnant; they figured I would become attached to him if we had a child. Fortunately I managed to have a birth control spiral fitted; they would have found out if I used pills. After a year, when I began behaving properly, we moved out to our own apartment. When two years had passed, I told him, 'Look, I do not intend to stay with you. Let's get a divorce.' He said he did not want me either. So we got a divorce, but my family was so upset that I now have no contact with them or most other Turks. I acquired a bad name. My brothers still follow and insult me for bringing shame to them. I am unable to visit the village in Turkey.

Battering is cause for divorce, as is a husband's financial irresponsibility such as gambling or using the wife's income for selfish reasons. There is also increasing intolerance of Western girlfriends of married Turkish men. Male promiscuity, which is rarely considered sufficient grounds for divorce in Turkey, was found to be an important factor leading to divorce among Turks in West Germany (Kudat and Frey, 1975). None of the nine divorced women in this study cited the extra-marital affairs of their husbands as a primary reason for their divorce; these were sometimes mentioned as contributing factors.

Women gave concrete reasons for seeking a divorce. Men offered less specific reasons, such as incompatibility and the difficulties of adjustment. Turkish men, traditionally, do not talk about their marriages. Divorced women are proud of their decision:

Now we are divorced. I am, for the first time in my life, at leisure.

I would have reconsidered if he had shown the least respect for me under pressure from his mother. He did not do that. I told him many times, I am not an animal. He would not understand. Now I feel human. I do not need a husband like that.

Men are upset by divorce, regarding it as an evil influence of European culture. A 25-year-old married man:

> Divorce is taken for granted (in Sweden), but it is not natural for us. Divorce can occur only if elders cannot solve the problems or if one of the partners has brought shame to the family. Problems which will arise after the divorce must be solved beforehand. The wife should go back to her parents and the man should take care of the children, for instance. They say a man has to pay for the woman after divorce. Swedes give privileges to women, but we cannot accept such things. (Akpinar, 1988)

A man divorced three times:

> One is afraid to bring Turkish women to this society. Here they take the stage and act as politicians. You have to applaud everything they do. They will not listen to what you say, they do whatever they want. This is what happens to the Turkish family [after migration]. (Akpinar, 1988)

In Turkey many people – relatives, neighbours and friends, community elders – intervene to dissuade couples from divorcing. This type of community involvement does not exist in Europe, where a family in crisis often seeks help from professionals who will often advise them to pursue divorce, rather than work out their differences. Turkish couples find this regrettable (Akpinar, 1988; Ertem-Kurtiz and Kuyumcu, 1985). Divorce collects a heavy toll from Turkish immigrants, and makes it even more difficult for the divorced man or woman to adjust to life in Europe.

Stereotypes

> The specific problems of immigrant women are a reality. At the same time, however, the debate on the 'problems' of immigrant women carries ideological undertones which in their consequences rarely benefit immigrant women themselves. Immigrant women find themselves successively protected and socialized into a self-image as vulnerable and in need of help; threatened by their subordinate positions in the labour market, their obsolete traditions, their cultural heritage, their men and their large families as well as their lifestyles and values. A very negative self-evaluation has developed. A wall of problem ideologies hinders women from clearly seeing themselves and their actual possibilities: their real limits but also their real resources (Ålund, 1988).

Some generalizations are unavoidable in the process of understanding any new culture. However, it is difficult to find a balance between stereotyping and giving credence to individual behaviour. When taken as absolute truth, generalizations carry the risk of producing stereotyped images of individuals. As it emphasizes differences, stereotyping carries the risk of ethnocentricity because differences are defined in relation to the norms of the dominant culture. Differences then become deviations, and deviations become 'problems'. Stereotyping carries with it the seeds of prejudice. When explaining in a TV programme why he thinks immigration should be discontinued, a Swedish youth says, in effect: '[the immigrant men's] attitude towards women is much different from ours. They consider women less than human. We cannot accept this.'

Whether immigrant men, more than other men, consider women inferior is open to discussion. However, as is true with many other groups of immigrants, Turks in Europe are acutely aware that in terms of gender roles, there is a strong tendency to stereotype Turkish men as unconditionally oppressive people. It is true that the attitudes of Turkish men towards women are different from those of Western men. This, however, is a truth with many subtleties and modifications: individuals vary. Statements to the effect that immigrant attitudes towards women are unacceptable put immigrant men in a difficult position: they must either abandon the values and conventions with which they feel morally secure, or be considered deviants in Western society. To secure a better life for themselves and their families, Turkish men have already abandoned their country, language, culture, occupation and social and political influence. Now they are made to feel that they should also leave behind the norms according to which they define themselves as dignified men and fathers, so they may be 'accepted'.

Pressure to change their attitudes towards women is perceived by Turkish men as a kind of emasculation, and a threat to the influence they still exercise over one area of their lives – their families. Their reaction to this pressure is one of indignation. A man from a rural town, in refusing to participate in this study, summarized his position as follows:

> What is there to discuss about my family? Write this: honour is that for which we live. Honour is all we have. Honour is all I and my wife will leave to our children. This will not change because we changed countries.

Turkish men recall their experiences:

> They think we all are violent, and batter children and women. It is frustrating to feel a need to tell people all the time that most of us in fact do not batter; that there is much affection and care in our families; that most of us actually would sacrifice our lives for our families.

> I sense suspicion whenever I meet someone for the first time, even though people are very polite. I feel as if the expression on people's faces changes when they hear I am a Turk. Maybe I am getting paranoid.

I told her to guess my nationality. She guessed: Canadian? French? Israeli? I told her I was a Turk. Without a word, she turned around and left me standing there alone, on the dance floor.

Many men have had similar humiliating experiences.

Women see the extent to which their men are humiliated, not only as disadvantaged competitors in the labour market, but more often because of their cultural baggage. In the debates concerning the problems of immigrant women, it is generally the men who are said to be the problem and who must change. It is men who have to confront outbursts of racist sentiment and sometimes violence. It is impossible for women to remain aloof from the pressures on their men. When the Turkish male is seen as an oppressor, the Turkish woman, by extension, becomes his victim:

There is an assumption that we Turkish women are bleeding under the oppression of fanatical, selfish, sexist male chauvinists. It is as if we must be rescued from our families and our men.

Such sentiments are shared by many groups of immigrant and minority women (Ålund, 1988; Carby, 1982; Hull *et al*, 1982). When confronted with stereotyped images, women react by increasing their loyalty to their men; no one understands the vulnerabilities of men living in an alien culture better than the women who also live in that culture.

Turkish men become more liberal in their attitudes to gender roles as they become more educated and their social status rises or as they find other areas in which they can exercise influence. Turkish immigrant men have been forced to leave behind their prospects for influence in all areas of life, with the exception of their family. Women have generally benefited from immigration as they have gained personal income and increased mobility without substantially affecting their traditional roles as mothers and wives. Women try to share these gains with their men to decrease the pressure on their men. They realize that as long as men are unable to compensate for their loss of influence, the power they have at home will remain of crucial importance in maintaining their feelings of male self-worth.

Because women want to stay with their families, they introduce change only in those areas which are directly related to smoother functioning of the family and better adjustment to the labour market. Women feel compelled to defend their culture as they also feel unfairly discriminated against and stereotyped:

Everybody at school used to tease us for being careful with boys and clothes. Other girls who were not interested in boys or clothes were not teased as we Turkish girls were.

I tell them I am divorced, and they say, 'Oh? Can Turkish women get divorced?' Then I feel I must explain all about our history, our rights, our society. It sometimes gets very frustrating.

I resent all this emphasis on the 'lack of freedom' of Turkish girls. Is it so terribly wrong not wanting to go to bed with the first boy who comes your way? Each time I participate in a study, a researcher begins asking about my sex life and whether somebody is oppressing it!

Generalizations that Turkish women are powerless do not imply that Turkish women are seen as deviants who ought to change in order to be accepted in Western society. But discrimination, whether negative or positive, distorts an individual and does not give him or her credit for having the same feelings as others. Turkish women often feel compelled to defend all the characteristics which define their culture, even if they may privately be critical of some of them. They resent and often reject the helping hand European society extends to them. They suspect that the outstretched hand may be motivated by ethnocentricity which seeks to rescue them from their 'archaic' culture, in order to bring Turkish women and their families to the same cultural platform as Western society.

Counter-stereotypes
Some years ago a woman confided to me a sad personal experience which made a lasting impression. This immigrant woman, who will be called Nesrin, had a husband who would some nights bring home Western women he had met at a dance restaurant and tell Nesrin to leave her bed and sleep in the living room, so that he and his guest could spend the night together. Nesrin would do as she was told.

There are several disturbing aspects of this story. It is not necessary to comment at length on the deplorable behaviour of the husband. It certainly is not typical of most Turkish men. Nesrin eventually obtained a divorce from him. What is more disturbing about this story is the behaviour of the women. A woman would not usually go into the home of another woman of the same nationality or culture, in the middle of the night to replace her in her bed and sleep with her husband. If such an unlikely thing were to happen, one would expect a confrontation to occur between the man's wife and his guest. Why did Nesrin never confront the women who came to her home? Why did the women who came not utter a word to Nesrin?

The answer is most disturbing: Nesrin did not wish to confront the women because she considered them too loose, too promiscuous, to be worthy of her attention. Did the non-Turkish interlopers think it was all right to violate a Turkish woman's home in such a way? Would they have agreed to accompany a man married to a Western woman to his home under similar circumstances? In fact, they accompanied the man to his home because they considered his Turkish wife to be too selfless, too lacking in pride, to be taken seriously. Thus, there was no dialogue between the women because each felt their reality was so removed from the other. But, are the realities of two women, who meet next to a man's bed, really so far apart? Is there nothing two women wish to communicate to one another, as one of them leaves her place in the bed to the other? What is the origin of the idea that the lives of Middle Eastern and

Western women are so different from one another that any attempt at dialogue is futile? In Nesrin's case, the husband was probably the source: he told Nesrin that non-Turkish women lack virtue and he told his girlfriends that Turkish women lack pride. Both women were exploited. The person who has access to information has the power to exploit, if it is desired, by using the information to mislead the unknowing and the insensitive.

The stereotyping of Turkish women as powerless victims of a patriarchy was discussed earlier. It is an extension of a larger phenomenon of stereotyping of all Muslim women as veiled and subordinated people with no rights or willpower. A glance at Western mass media confirms this: most articles about Muslim society are accompanied by pictures of veiled women, a fearful sight for Western women as they suggest the absence of that which Western women have struggled for, for so many decades.

Turks are not immune from ethnocentricity, producing their own stereotypical images attempting to highlight differences, set limits and justify the superiority of their cultural norms. A recent study of the image of Western society in the Turkish daily newspapers reveals stereotyped images. The press depicted the Western family as a deteriorating institution with high divorce rates, fatherless homes, incest, child and drug abuse. The Western male is portrayed as powerless and emasculated, unable to commit himself to a woman or to raising a family. The Western woman is portrayed as a careerist with a great appetite for unrestrained sex, also unable to commit herself to a monogamous relationship and unable to be a devoted mother. Most such accounts are accompanied by pictures of nearly-naked women (A. Kocturk, 1987).

These generalizations about Western lifestyles are not confined to Turkey, but are true of most Middle Eastern/Muslim societies (Azari, 1983; El-Saadawi, 1980). When Turkish immigrants, regardless of background or social class, consistently state that they regard their own norms of family and gender roles as superior to the West, they are expressing a desire to distance themselves from the image outlined above, which terrifies the Turkish/Muslim woman as much as the picture of the veiled woman terrifies her Western sister. When looking at the half-naked woman's picture, the Muslim woman feels grateful that her culture does not, at least, expose women in such a way. She may even think that, despite shortcomings, the Muslim patriarchy is possibly better than others.

Stereotypes produce counter-stereotypes which reinforce the walls of prejudice and suffocate the prospects for human communication. A barrier is erected when a subordinated, private and veiled woman is contrasted to a liberated, public and naked woman – one of them does not have equal rights, but is respected; the other has equal rights, but not much respectability (Youssef, 1974). This is akin to the Madonna/whore duality, which has confused and divided women throughout the ages. There is a need to be more sensitive to the anxieties that these images evoke in the female subconscious. The image of the veiled, subordinated woman suggests to the Western woman that she should be satisfied with, and grateful for, the rights she has and not demand more. The image of the naked woman whispers to the Muslim that she should not insist on getting too many rights, unless she wants to lose her virtue. The reality, of course, is that Muslim women are not absolutely powerless, lacking personal pride and control over their lives, any more than Western women completely lack virtue and standards of sexual conduct.

When, and if, people – especially women – begin searching beyond the stereotypes, they will be able to reach a higher level of understanding and collaborate with one another to change the condition of human relationships. The objective of women's emancipation is not only a struggle for equal rights. Neither is it only a struggle to acquire or retain respectability. Women all over the world want both rights and respect. Instead of being forced to sacrifice one for the other, or instead of wasting precious time questioning which is a more preferable patriarchal system, this goal should unite women to induce change.

References

Abadan-Unat, N. (1964), *Bati Almanya'daki Turk iscileri ve sorunlari* (Turkish workers in West Germany and their problems. In Turkish), State Planning Organization: Ankara.

Abadan-Unat, N. (1982), 'The effect of international labor migration on women's roles: the Turkish case', in *Sex Roles, Family and Community in Turkey,* C. Kagitcibasi (ed.), Indiana University: Bloomington.

Abadan-Unat, N. (1986), 'The legal status of Turkish women', in *The Study of Women in Turkey* F. Özbay (ed.), UNESCO/Turkish Social Science Association: Ankara.

Afetinan, A. (1982), *Tarih Boyunca Turk Kadininin Hak ve Görevleri* (The rights and duties of Turkish women throughout history. In Turkish), Milli Egitim: Istanbul.

Ahmed, L. (1982), 'Feminism and feminist movements in the Middle East, a preliminary exploration: Turkey, Egypt, Algeria, People's Democratic Republic of Yemen', *Women's Studies International Forum*, 5, pp. 153-168.

Aker, A. (1972), *Isci göcu: Nisan 1970 ile Nisan 1971 arasinda Almanya'ya giden Turk iscileri uzerinde sosyo-ekonomik bir örnekleme arastirmasi* (Labour migration: a socioeconomic sample study on Turkish workers who emigrated to Germany between April 1970 and 1971. In Turkish), Sander: Istanbul.

Akiner, S. (1986), *Islamic Peoples of the Soviet Union,* London.

Akpinar, A. (1987), 'Migrant families in crisis', Swedish Institute for Social Research, Stockholm University: Stockholm, unpublished report.

Akpinar, A. (1988), *Invandrarfamiljer i kris* (Immigrant families in crisis. In Swedish), Svenska insututet för social forskning, Stockholm University: Stockholm, unpublished report.

Alpay, S. (1980), 'Turkar i Stockholm' (Turks in Stockholm. In Swedish), Stockholm Studies in Politics, 16, Liber: Stockholm.

Al-Tibri, A. (1982), 'A study of Islamic her-story: or how did we ever get into this mess?', *Women's Studies International Forum*, 5, pp. 207-219.

Ålund, A. (1988), 'Etnocentrism i problemideologin', I *Konfliktlösning i det flerkulturella samhället,* (Ethnocentrism in the problem ideology. In: Conflict solving in the multicultural society. In Swedish), G. Winai-Ström (ed.), Uppsala University: Uppsala.

Antes, P. (1985), 'Islamic identity and the Turks in West Germany', in *Muslims in Germany-German Muslims? Questions of Identity,* J.S. Nielsen (ed.), The Centre for the Study of Islam and Christian-Muslim Relations, Selly Oak College: Birmingham, research papers.

Armstrong, K. (1987), *The Gospel According to Woman,* Pan: London.

Aronowitz, A. (1988), 'Accumulation and deliquency among second generation Turkish youths in Berlin', *Migration,* 4, pp. 5-36.

Avcioglu, D. (1987), *Turklerin Tarihi* (The history of Turks. In Turkish): Istanbul.

Azari, F. (1983), *Women of Iran: The conflict with fundamentalist Islam,* Ithaca London.

Bagir, herkes duysun, (Shout, so everybody hears. In Turkish) (1988), Kadin Cevresi: Istanbul.

Bakhtiyar, L. (1987), *Sufi: Expressions of the Mystic Quest,* Thames and Hudson: Singapore.

Balaman, A. R. (1985), 'Family formation and dissolution in rural areas', in *Family in Turkish Society,* T. Erder (ed.), Turkish Social Science Association: Ankara.

Baysal, A. (1979), 'Turk kadinin beslenme sorunlari', (Nutritional problems of Turkish women), in *Turk toplumunda kadin* (Women in Turkish society), N. Abadan-Unat (ed.), Sosyal Bilimler Dernegi: Ankara.

Bendix, J. (1985), 'On the rights of foreign workers in West Germany', in *Turkish Workers in Europe,* I. Basgöz and N. Furniss (eds.), Indiana University: Bloomington.

Bergman, B. (1987) 'Battered wives: why are they beaten and why do they stay?' Karolinska Institutet: Stockholm, PhD thesis.

Bergman, E. and B. Svedin (1982), 'Vittnesmål: Invandrares syn på diskriminering i Sverige', (Testimony: immigrants' views on discrimination in Sweden. In Swedish), Liber: Stockholm.

Bingöllu-Sayari, B. (1979), 'Turk Kadini ve Din' (The Turkish woman and religion. In Turkish) in *Turk toplumunda kadin* (Women in Turkish society), N. Abadan-Unat (ed.), Sosyal Bilimler Dernegi: Ankara.

Boratav, P. N. (1985), 'The folklore of Turkish immigrant workers in France', in *Turkish Workers in Europe,* I. Basgöz and N. Furniss (eds.), Indiana University: Bloomington.

Boudhiba, A. (1985), *Sexuality in Islam,* trans. A. Sheridan, Routledge & Kegan Paul: London.

Bowles, G. T. (1977), *The People of Asia,* Weidenfeld and Nicolson: London.

Brill, E. J. (ed.) (1960), *Encyclopaedia of Islam,* Leiden, the Netherlands.

Caporal, B. (1982), *Kemalizmde ve Kemalizm sonrasinda Turk kadini* (Turkish women in Kemalism. In Turkish), Is Bankasi Yay: Ankara.

Carby, H. (1982), 'White woman listen: Black feminism and the boundaries of sisterhood', in *The Empire Strikes Back,* Centre for Contemporary Cultural Studies: London.

Castles, S., H. Booth and T. Wallace (1984), *Here for Good,* Pluto: London.

Citci, O. (1986), 'Women in public sector', in *The Study of Women in Turkey: an anthology,* F. Özbay (ed.), UNESCO/Turkish Social Science Association: Ankara.

Culpan, O. and T. Marzotti (1982), 'Changing attitudes toward work and marriage: Turkey in transition', *Signs,* Winter, pp. 337-51.

Davis, J. D. and B. Sherman Heyl (1986), 'Turkish women and guestworker migration to West Germany', in *International Migration: the female experience,* R. J. Simon and C. B. Bretell (eds.), Rowman and Allanheld: New Jersey.

Demircan, A. R. (1985), *Islam'a göre cinsel hayat* (Sexual life according to Islam. In Turkish), Eymen: Istanbul.

Dodd, P. C. (1973), 'Family honour and forces of change in Arab society', *Int. J. Middle Eastern Studies,* 4, pp. 42-47.

Duben, A. (1985), 'Nineteenth and twentieth century Ottoman-Turkish family and household structures', in *Family in Turkish Society,* T. Erder (ed.), Turkish Social Science Association: Ankara.

Dubetsky, A. (1977), 'Class and community in urban Turkey', in *Commoners, Climbers and Notables: social ranking in the Middle East,* C. van Nieuwenhuijze (ed.), E. J. Brill: Leiden.

Ejerfeldt, L. (1988), 'Islam i Sverige' (Islam in Sweden. In Swedish), in *Det Mångkulturella Sverige* (Multicultural Sweden). I. Svanberg and H. Runblom (eds.), Gidlunds: Stockholm.

El-Saadawi, N. (1980), *The Hidden Face of Eve: women in the Arab world,* Zed Press: London.

Ergun-Engström, G. and A. Heyman (1989), *Barnuppfostran och kulturmöten: Att växa upp i Turkiet och Sverige,* (Childrearing and cultural meetings. Growing up in Turkey and Sweden. In Swedish), Författares bokmaskin: Stockholm.

Erkut, S. (1982), 'Dualism in values toward education of Turkish women', in *Sex Roles, Family and the Community in Turkey,* C. Kagitcibasi (ed.), Indiana University: Bloomington.

Ertem-Kurtiz, G. and E. Kuyumcu (1985), *Turkiska kvinnor i myndighetssverige,* (Turkish women and Swedish authorities. In Swedish), Statens invandrarverk: Norrköping.

Fahri, I. (1984), *Toplumumuzda kadin ve cinsellik* (Woman and sexuality in society. In Turkish), Altin kitaplar: Istanbul.

Fallers, L. A. and M. C. Fallers (1976), 'Sex roles in Edremit', in *Mediterranean Family Structures,* J. G. Peristiany (ed.), Cambridge University Press: Cambridge.

Fisher, W. B. (1983), 'Turkey', in *The Middle East and North Africa 1983-84,* Europa: London.

Gökalp, A. (1980), 'Une minorité Chitte en Anatolie: les Alevi' (A Shiite minority in Anatolia: the Alevi. In French), *Annales Economies, Sociétés, Civilisations,* 3, pp. 739-763.

Gölpinarli, A. (1963), *Alevi-Bektasi Nefesleri* (Alevi-Bektashi songs. In Turkish), Remzi: Istanbul.

'Good News' *New Testament,* Collins/Fount: Glasgow. (1976 edition)

Graham-Brown, S. (1988), *Images of Women: The portrayal of women in photography of the Middle East 1860-1950,* Quartet: London.

Guneng, H. (1987), 'Underordnad i livet-likställd efter döden', (Subordinate in life – equal after death. In Swedish), in *Kön, makt, medborgarskap,* M. Eduards (ed.), Liber: Malmö.

Hacettepe University (1989), Institute of Population Studies, 1988 Turkish Population and Health Survey: Ankara.

Halman, T. S. (1985), 'Big town blues: peasants "abroad" in Turkish literature', in *Turkish Workers in Europe,* I. Basgöz and N. Furniss (eds.), Indiana University: Bloomington.

Hassan, U. (1985), *Eski Turk Toplumu Uzerine Incelemeler* (Studies on Ancient Turkish Society. In Turkish): Istanbul.

Hedenborg, J. (1839), *Turkiska nationens seder, bruk och klädedrägter* (The traditions, customs and clothing of the Turkish nation. In Swedish): Stockholm.

Hela världen i fakta '88 (The whole world in facts. In Swedish), Bonniers: Stockholm.

Hjärpe, J. (1983), *Islam: Lära och livsmönster,* (Islam: teaching and life patterns. In Swedish), Almquist & Wiksell: Stockholm.

Hjärpe, J. (1984), *Politisk Islam* (Political Islam. In Swedish), Skeab: Stockholm.

Horner, M. S. (1972), 'Toward an understanding of achievement-related conflicts', *J. Social Issues,* 28, pp. 157-72.

Hull, G., P. Bell Scott, B. Smith (eds.) (1982), *All the Women are White, All the Men are Black, but Some of Us are Brave,* Feminist Press: New York.

Ibn Battuta (1958), *The Travels of Ibn Battuta AD 1325–54,* trans. H. A. R. Gibb, Cambridge.

Jeppesen, K. J. (1989), *Unge Invandrare* (Young immigrants. In Danish). Socialforskningsinstitutet: Copenhagen.

Jonung, C. (1982), *Migrant Women in the Swedish Labor Market,* Commission for Immigration Research: Stockholm.

Kagitcibasi, C. (1981), *Cocugun degeri: Turkiye' de degerler ve dogurganlik,* (The value of the child: values and fertility in Turkey), Bogazici University: Istanbul.

Kagitcibasi, C. (1986), 'Women's intra-family status in Turkey: cross-cultural perspectives', in *The Study of Women in Turkey: an anthology,* F. Özbay (ed.), UNESCO/Social Science Association: Ankara.

Kagitcibasi, C. (1987), 'Alienation of the outsider: the plight of migrants', *International Migration* 25, pp. 195-210.

Kandiyoti, D. (1977), 'Sex roles and social change: a comparative appraisal of Turkish women', *Signs,* 3, pp. 57-73.

Kandiyoti, D. (1979), 'Kadinlarda psiko-sosyal degisim: Kusaklar arasinda bir karsilastirma' (Psychosocial change in women: an intergenerational comparison. In Turkish) in *Turk toplumunda kadin* (Women in Turkish society), Sosyat Bilimler Dernegi: Ankara. N. Abadan-Unat (ed.).

Kaplan, I. (1985), 'Provisions related to the protection of the family in labor, social security and health laws', in *Family in Turkish Society,* T. Erder (ed.), Turkish Social Science Association: Ankara.

Karpat, K. (1976), *The Gecekondu: Rural migration and urbanization,* Cambridge University Press: Cambridge.

Kinross, P. B. (1964), *Ataturk: the rebirth of a nation,* London.

Kiray, M. (1986), 'The family of the immigrant worker', in *The Study of Women in Turkey: an anthology,* F. Özbay (ed.), UNESCO/Turkish Social Science Association: Istanbul.

Kocturk, A. (1987), 'Turk basininda bati' (The West in the Turkish press. In Turkish). Middle East Technical University: Ankara, unpublished paper.

Kocturk, T. (1988a), 'Heder, identitet och islam', in *Konfliktlösning i det flerkulturella samhället* (Honour, identity and Islam. In: Conflict solving in the multicultural society. In Swedish), G. Winai-Ström (ed.), Uppsala University: Uppsala.

Kocturk, T. (1988b), 'Options and strategies of Turkish immigrant women', unpublished paper.

Kocturk-Runefors, T. (1988), 'Options and strategies of Turkish immigrant women', unpublished paper.

Kongar, E. (1979), *Turkiye'nin toplumsal yapisi,* (The social structure of Turkey. In Turkish): Istanbul.

The Koran, trans. N. J. Dawood, Penguin: Middlesex (1974 edition).

Kudat, A. and F. Frey (1975), 'Stability and change in the Turkish family at home and abroad: comparative perspectives', Wissenschaftszentrum: Berlin, unpublished paper.

Kuran-i Kerim ve Turkce tefsirli meal-i alisi, trans. E. Baytan, (The glorious Koran and its interpreted contents in Turkish), Baytan: Istanbul (1987 edition).

Kuyas, A. (1982), 'Female labour power relations in the urban Turkish family', in *Sex Roles, Family and the Community in Turkey,* C. Kagitcibasi (ed.), Indiana University: Bloomington.

Leiniö, T-L. (1988), 'Giftermål och skilsmässor bland finlänska, jugoslaviska och turkiska invandrare mellan 1971 och 1984' (Marriage and divorce among Finnish, Yugoslavian and Turkish immigrants between 1971 and 1984. In

Swedish), in *Invandrade kvinnor i Norden,* Arbetsmarknadsdepartementet, jämställdhetsenheten: Stockholm.

Liljeström, R. (1982) *Det erotiska kriget* (The erotic war. In Swedish), Liber: Stockholm.

Lithman, Y. G. (1988), 'Social relations and cultural continuities: Muslim immigrants and their social networks', in *The New Islamic Presence in Europe,* T. Gerholm and Y.G. Lithman (eds.), Mansell: London.

Magnarella, P. J. (1974), *Tradition and Change in a Turkish Town,* John Wiley and Sons: New York.

Magnarella, P. J. (1979), *The Peasant Venture,* Schenkman: Cambridge, Massachusetts.

Maillat, D. (1986), *The Future of Migration: the experience of European receiving countries,* OECD: Paris.

Månsson, S-A. (1984), *Kärlek och kulturkonflikt* (Love and cultural conflict. In Swedish), Prisma/Socialstyrelsen: Arlöv.

Mardin, S. (1983), *Din ve ideoloji* (Religion and ideology), Iletisim: Istanbul.

Menges, K. (1968), *The Turkic Languages and Peoples:* London.

Merdol (Kocturk-Runefors), T. (1982), *Turkish Women: background and living conditions,* Statens invandrarverk: Norrköping.

Mernissi, F. (1985), *Beyond the Veil: male-female dynamics in a Muslim society,* Al Saqi: London.

Mikhailovsky, V. H. (1984), *Shamanism in Siberia and European Russia* (trans. O. Wardrop), New York.

Montagu (1898), *The Letters and Works of Lady Mary Wortley Montagu,* Bohns Standard Library, 2 vols.: London.

Mortensen, L. B. (1989), 'Familien för Allah-Tyrkiske invandrerkvinder i Kopenhavn' (The family for Allah-Turkish immigrant women in Copenhagen. In Danish), in *Muslimska kvinnor i Norden* (Muslim women in Nordic countries), B. Ornbrant (ed.), DEIFO, Rapport No.11: Stockholm.

Mortensen, L. B. (1990), 'Arbejde: den tyrkiske kvindes belonning er hjemmet', (Work: the Turkish woman's gift is her home. In Danish). Report to the Seminar on Immigrant Women in Nordic Countries: Copenhagen (February).

Müftüoglu, M. A. (trans.) (1981), *Gazali: Ihyau 'ulumi'd Din* (Revivification of religious sciences. In Turkish), Cile: Istanbul.

Naess, R. (1988), 'Being an Alevi Muslim in south-western Anatolia and in Norway: the impact of migration on a heterodox Turkish community, in *The New Islamic Presence in Europe,* T. Gerholm and Y. Lithman (eds.), Mansell: London.

Nauck, B. (1989), 'Assimilation process and group integration of migrant families', *International Migration,* 27, pp. 27-48.

Nordberg, M. (1988), *Profetens Folk: stat, samhälle och kultur i Islam under tusen år* (The people of the prophet. State, society and culture in Islam during a thousand years. In Swedish), Tiden: Stockholm.

Olson, E. A. (1985a), 'Duofocal family structure and an alternative model of husband-wife relationships', in *Sex Roles, Family and Community in Turkey*, C. Kagitcibasi (ed.), Indiana University: Bloomington.

Olson, E. A. (1985b), 'Muslim identity and secularism in contemporary Turkey: "the headscarf dispute"', *Anthropological Quarterly*, 58, pp. 161-71.

Öncu, A. (1979), 'Uzman mesleklerde Turk kadini', in *Turk toplumunda kadin*, N. Abadan-Unat, D. Kandiyoti, M. Kiray (eds.), Turkish Social Science Association: Ankara.

Ortayli, I. (1985), 'The family in Ottoman society', in *Family in Turkish Society: sociological and legal studies*, T. Erder (ed.): Ankara.

Özbay, F. (1982), 'Women's education in rural Turkey', in *Sex Roles, Family and Community in Turkey*, C. Kagitcibasi (ed.), Indiana University: Bloomington.

Özbay, F. (1986), 'Development of studies on women in Turkey', in *The Study of Women in Turkey: an anthology*, F. Özbay (ed.), UNESCO/Turkish Social Science Association: Ankara.

Özek, C. (1988), *Devlet ve din* (State and religion. In Turkish), Ada: Istanbul.

Özgur, S. and D. Sunar (1982), 'Social psychological patterns of homicide in Turkey: A comparison of male and female convicted murderers', in *Sex Roles, Family and Community in Turkey*, C. Kagitcibasi (ed.), Indiana University: Bloomington.

Paine, S. (1974), *Exporting Workers: the Turkish case*, Cambridge University Press: Cambridge.

Pavic, M. (1988), *Kazarisk uppslagsbok* (Khazarian reference book. In Swedish): Stockholm.

Peristiany, J. G. (ed.) (1965), *Honour and Shame: the values of Mediterranean society*, Weidenfeld and Nicolson: London.

Petek-Salom, G. and P. Hüküm (1986), 'Women's emancipation after the Atatürk Period', in *Women of the Mediterranean*, M. Gadant (ed.), Zed Books: London.

Quastana, A. M. and S. Casanova (1986), 'Women and Corsican identity', in *Women of the Mediterranean*, M. Gadant (ed.), Zed Books: London.

'Raise your voice' (Sesini yukselt), Proceedings of the Conference on Turkish Immigrant Women, Amsterdam, 6–8 June, 1985.

Ringgren, H. and Å. V. Åström (1978), 'Islam', in *Religionerna i historia och nutid* (Religions in history and in the present. In Swedish), Verbum: Stockholm.

Sachs, L. (1983), 'Evil eye or bacteria: Turkish immigrant women and Swedish health care', Monograph, Department of Social Anthropology, Stockholm University: Stockholm.

Sachs, L. (1984), *Heder och skam: Om sociala relationer i Medelhavsområdet* (Honour and shame. On social relations in the Mediterranean region. In Swedish). Socialstyrelsen redovisar: Stockholm.

Safilios-Rothschild, C. (1969), 'Honour crimes in contemporary Greece', *British Journal of Sociology,* 20, pp. 205-18.

Safilios-Rotschild, C. (1971), 'A cross-cultural examination of women's marital, educational and occupational options', *Acta Sociologia,* 14, pp. 93-113.

Sander, Å. (1988a), *Muslimer i Europa – enskilda länder* (Muslims in Europe – individual countries. In Swedish), Institution för Filosofi, Göteborgs Universitet: Gothenburg.

Sander, Å. (1988b), *Kan Koranskolan fungera som medium för traditions – förmedling?* (Can Koran schools function as mediators of tradition? In Swedish), KIM-Rapport No.11, Institutionen för Filosofi, Göteborgs Universitet: Gothenburg.

Schaps, D. M. (1979), *Economic Rights of Women in Ancient Greece*: Edinburgh.

Schimmel, A. M. (1982), 'Women in mystical Islam', *Women's Studies International Forum,* 5, pp. 145-151.

School, J. J. (1984), 'Fertility and age at marriage of Turkish women in the Netherlands', *Turkish Journal of Population Studues,* 6, pp. 27-47.

Sen, F. (1990), 'Problems and integration constraints of Turkish migrants in the Federal Republic of Germany', World Employment Programme, Working paper No.44, ILO: Geneva.

Senyapili, T. (1978), *Butunlesmemis kentli nufus sorunu* (The problem of unintegrated urban population. In Turkish). Middle East Technical University: Ankara.

Severy, M. and J.L. Stanfield (1987), 'Suleyman the magnificent', *National Geographic,* 172 (5), pp. 552-601.

Similä, M. (1987), *Kulturell identitet hos unga invandrare* (Cultural identity in young immigrants. In Swedish), Stockholm Universitet: Stockholm.

Slomp, J. (1988), 'Muslim minorities in the Netherlands. Muslims in Europe', Research Paper 37, Centre for the Study of Islam and Christian-Muslim Relations, Selly Oak Colleges: Birmingham.

Smith, J. and Y. Haddad (1982), 'Eve: the Islamic image of woman', *Women's Studies International Forum,* 5, pp. 135-144.

Soysal, S. (1976), *Baris adli cocuk* (Child called Peace. In Turkish), Bilgi: Ankara.

Stadling, J. (1912), *Schamanismen i Norra Asien* (Shamanism in North Asia. In Swedish): Stockholm.

Stirling, P. (1965), *Turkish Village,* Weidenfeld and Nicolson: London.

Stiver Lie, S. (1985), 'Turkish migrant women and wage labour: A comparative study of Turkish migrant women's employment in West Germany, The Netherlands, Great Britain, Sweden and Norway', paper presented at the European Conference of Turkish Women Migrants: Amsterdam.

Svanberg, I. (1985), 'Invandrare från Turkiet: Etnisk och sociokulturell variation', (Immigrants from Turkey: Ethnic and sociocultural variation. In Swedish). Uppsala Multi-ethnic Papers, 4, Uppsala University: Uppsala.

Tasiran, H. (1989), 'Invandrade kvinnor från Turkiet i Göteborg och London', (Immigrant women from Turkey in Göteborg and London. In Swedish). Göteborg University: Götenburg, unpublished paper.

Taskiran, T. (1973), *Cumhuriyetin 50. yilinda Turk kadin haklari* (Turkish women's rights on the 50th anniversary of the republic. In Turkish), Basbakanlik Kultur Mustesarligi: Ankara.

Tekeli, S. (1982), *Kadinlar ve siyasal toplumsal hayat* (Women and political-social life. In Turkish), Birikim: Istanbul.

Tekeli, S. (1986), 'The meaning and limits of feminist ideology in Turkey', in *The Study of Women in Turkey,* F. Özbay (ed.), UNESCO/Turkish Social Science Association: Ankara.

Thomä-Venske, H. (1988), 'The religious life of Muslims in Berlin', in *The New Islamic Presence in Europe,* T. Gerholm and Y. Lithman (eds.), Mansell: London.

Timur, S. (1979), 'Turkiye'de aile yapisinin belirleyicileri', (The determinants of family structure in Turkey. İn Turkish), in *Turk toplumunda kadin* (Women in Turkish Society), N. Abadan-Unat (ed.), Sosyal Bilimer Dernegi: Ankara.

Toelken, B. (1985), '"Turkenrein" and "Turken, raus!" – Images of fear and aggression in German Gastarbeiterwitze', in *Turkish Workers in Europe,* I. Basgöz and N. Furniss (eds.), Indiana University, Bloomington.

Toynbee, A. (1964), *Le monde et l'occident:* Paris.

Tuglaci, P. (1984), *Women of Istanbul in Ottoman Times,* Cem: Istanbul.

Ulku, H. (1982), *Baslangictan gunumuze kadar Islam tarihi* (Islam history from the beginning to today. In Turkish). Cile: Istanbul.

Utrio, K. (1987), *Evas döttrar: Kvinnans, barnets och familjens historia i Europa,* (The daughters of Eve. A story of the history of the woman's, child's, and family's history in Europe. In Swedish), Prisma: Stockholm.

Wilpert, C. (1988), 'Religion and ethnicity: orientations, perceptions and strategies among Turkish Alevi and Sunni migrants in Berlin', in *The New Islamic Presence in Europe,* T. Gerhold and Y. Lithman (eds.), Mansell: London.

Woodsmall, R. F. (1936), *Moslem Women Enter a New World,* Round Table: New York.

Yazgan, A. (1983), *Turkiska flickor* (Turkish girls. In Swedish), Statens invandrarverk: Norrköping.

Youssef, N. (1974), 'Women's status and fertility in Muslim countries of the Middle East and Asia', paper submitted to the Symposium on Woman's Status and Fertility Around the World, American Psychological Association, August, 1974: New Orleans.

Index